Teaching Success Guide for the Advanced Placement Classroom

Advanced Placement Classroom

A Midsummer Night's Dream

Advanced Placement Classroom

A Midsummer Night's Dream

Kathryn L. Johnson and Laurie Heineman

PRUFROCK PRESS INC.
WACO, TEXAS

Library of Congress Cataloging-in-Publication Data

Johnson, Kathryn L.
  A midsummer night's dream / Kathryn L. Johnson and Laurie Heineman.
    p. cm.—(Teaching success guide for the advanced placement classroom)
  At head of title on cover: Advanced placement classroom.
  Includes bibliographical references.
  ISBN-13: 978-1-59363-354-7 (pbk.)
  ISBN-10: 1-59363-354-8 (pbk.)
  1. Shakespeare, William, 1564–1616. Midsummer night's dream. 2. Shakespeare, William, 1564–1616—Study and teaching. I. Heineman, Laurie. II. Title.
  PR2827.J64 2009
  822.3'3—dc22
                              2008031590

Copyright ©2009 Prufrock Press Inc.

Edited by Lacy Elwood
Production Design by Marjorie Parker
Photographs by Debra Page-Trim and Laurie Heineman

ISBN-13: 978-1-59363-354-7
ISBN-10: 1-59363-354-8

At the time of this book's publication, all facts and figures cited are the most current available; all telephone numbers, addresses, and Web site URLs are accurate and active; all publications, organizations, Web sites, and other resources exist as described in this book; and all have been verified. The authors and Prufrock Press make no warranty or guarantee concerning the information and materials given out by organizations or content found at Web sites, and we are not responsible for any changes that occur after this book's publication. If you find an error or believe that a resource listed here is not as described, please contact Prufrock Press.

•AP and Advanced Placement Program are registered trademarks of the College Entrance Examination Board, which was not involved in the production of, and does not endorse, this book.

Prufrock Press Inc.
P.O. Box 8813
Waco, TX 76714-8813
Phone: (800) 998-2208
Fax: (800) 240-0333
http://www.prufrock.com

Contents

Acknowledgements

To the students who earnestly perform Shakespeare; to Bobbie Sanders, who recited lines of Shakespeare by heart (and with heart!) for any occasion, and mentored me in the writing process; to Mary Manning, who brought the joy of acting Shakespeare to my sons in eighth grade and began their lifelong love of the Bard; to the three men in my life, Jacob, Cliff, and Paul, who cast a magic spell on me every day!—KLJ

Forever thanks to all of the great actors, directors, and students who inspire me; to Albert Cullum who brought his touch of greatness into my fifth-grade classroom and set me on my life's path. For Tresa Hughes and Leland Moss, each of you "held the mirror up to nature" with immense honesty. My parents Frank and Uki, and my sisters Helen and Carol—you showed me alternate ways to approach life and to celebrate the whole spectrum. And, love to dearest girls Annie and Yulan, and to Ron who always makes it possible.—LH

Introduction and Getting Ready to Read *A Midsummer Night's Dream*

Stir up the Athenian youth to merriments.
—Theseus (Act I, scene i, line 13)

Introduction

We study Shakespeare to make lifelong friends who leap off the page, onto the stage, and into our lives. Always remember that Shakespeare wrote his plays for the human voice, speaking and acting upon the stage, so as we approach *A Midsummer Night's Dream* (which we often will refer to as *MSND*), let us think of ourselves as players as well as readers. Let us stir up your students to merriment—to that great merriment of luscious language, vivid imagery, and characters who will live with you for the rest of your lives.

William Shakespeare was born in England in April of 1564, and 52 years later, died in April of 1616. In between he married, had children, left his home in Stratford, went to London, and became an actor and playwright. He didn't leave many biographical markers, just the indelible marks of the masterpieces he wrote. He was a brilliant craftsman, a profound thinker, a witty storyteller, a wildly hilarious comic writer, a heart-throbbing romantic, a heartbreaking tragedian, and a practical man of the theater whose plays have been performed continuously for more than 400 years.

Come, enter the magical forest of *A Midsummer Night's Dream*!

Overview of Shakespeare and His Plays

Shakespeare's art came alive during the reign of Elizabeth I. This third monarch among the children of Henry VIII longed for peace and prosperity after the turbulent years of religious strife during previous reigns. Elizabeth I oversaw the largest flowering of peacetime theatrical creativity in all of England's history and Will Shakespeare arrived in London at the right time (Greenblatt, 2004).

The fact that Shakespeare's plays continue to live on the stage and the page is a great tribute to his characters, his gripping and sometimes uproarious plots of human passion and frailty, and his beautiful and powerful use of language. Shakespeare created characters that are both universal and specifically individual, one major key to longevity in theatrical literature. For example, Nick Bottom is a particular character with his own personal attributes; with his enormous ego, his mistaken word usage, and his good-heartedness, and because he is so much himself, we are able to see those character traits and foibles in ourselves and in those we know. He is a mirror of humanity in his individuality. This gift for creating specificity and universality is an enormous part of what made Shakespeare a great playwright and showman, and keeps his work relevant today.

Shakespeare didn't write "classics." He wrote plays for a broad audience that were immensely popular in his own time and have since become classics. Describing Shakespeare's audience, the great director Peter Brook said,

> He didn't have a lot of quiet, attentive people in a dark room . . . It was, rather, the most mixed audience that ever existed in the theater: thieves, pickpockets, whores, drunks, half-drunks, brawling in fights. As well of course as the bourgeoisie, there for entertainment, sophisticates looking for things that are sharp, witty, erudite. It is difficult to understand how deeply *difficult* the task was: Shakespeare at every moment had to bring *all* those along. Because if you learn anything from the theater it's that if you lose part of an audience, you're *dead*. The work is to bring them all together into one organism beating with one heart . . . (Rosenbaum, 2006, p. 372)

Shakespeare managed to juggle all of those varied audience desires at once and create magic in his works.

Ideas, images, sounds, and themes that arise in *MSND* and in Shakespeare's other works can amaze and delight us on first view. Then, the power deepens as they reemerge, and circle around again, more profound and significant with each viewing. As students read this play they will find that certain facets become more meaningful and/or more humorous every time they are encountered. Hopefully, this first meeting with *MSND* will not be your students' last and they will fall in love with Shakespeare. One hopes that on each rereading they will join in asking the question that Rosenbaum (2006) posed in his intriguing book, *The Shakespeare Wars*, "This to me is one of the wonders and enigmas: is there no end, no bottom to Shakespearean resonances?" (p. 20).

Students may bring up long-standing controversies and questions about the authorship of Shakespeare's plays. What a pleasure to be joining in a conversation that has been going on for hundreds of years. Some posit that such a minimally educated young man from Stratford couldn't have had the finesse to write the brilliant poetry of the plays. Others counter that a well-educated member of the nobility would never have been as familiar with the world of nature as this country boy from Stratford who made so many glorious allusions to flowers, weather, and folk tales. As students read this play, you may ask them to notice the rich and varied references to natural environments and the witty, poetic language.

About *A Midsummer Night's Dream*

A Midsummer Night's Dream is one of Shakespeare's most loved and frequently performed comedies. It has been played nonstop for more than 400 years because of its universal appeal as a romantic comedy with slapstick elements that enhance its humorous effect. *MSND* encompasses three worlds: the orderly royal court of Athens, the magical fairy world, and the world of the common working people. The irrational forces of passion invade all three worlds. The theme, "the course of true love never did run smooth" (I, i, 136) is central. Theseus and Hippolyta, characters from mythic Greece, appear here as a couple about to marry, a couple whose degree of passion for each other is not evenly matched at the beginning of the play. They are warriors who have fought against each other and the conqueror is wedding the vanquished—who has vanquished his heart. Hermia and Helena, who were girlhood friends, become allies and then rivals for Lysander and Demetrius. Their love triangles have all of the melodrama of young love, and their powerful emotions encompass both heartbreak and humor. Oberon and Titania, rulers of the nighttime magical forest also are out of tune in love and like all of the couples in this romantic romp, they are thrown off course by eruptions of jealousy, confusion, and passion. The fairy kingdom introduces the symbol of the irrational aspects of love with a magic flower whose juice makes one mad for love. Even the workingmen of Athens add a vision of irrational love with their play of star-crossed lovers. All of these worlds, and all of these facets of passion will be explored in this book.

The famously hilarious play-within-the-play, "The most lamentable comedy and most cruel death of Pyramus and Thisbe" (I, ii, 11–13) is about young love that ends badly when mistakes of understanding lead to suicide and death. This play-within-the-play shares an important plot element with *Romeo and Juliet*, when one lover, thinking the other is dead, kills himself. There is a general consensus that *Romeo and Juliet* was first performed in 1594, and *MSND* in 1595, but the writing of the two may have overlapped. This is another example of Shakespeare's brilliance, to take the same material and by viewing it from different points of view, create a heartbreaking tragedy and a sidesplitting comedy.

The midsummer night of the title refers to the summer solstice, the longest day of the year that occurs around June 22. In pagan times this season of the earth's renewed fertility was the basis for tribal festivities that lasted the whole night. It was part of folk knowledge that this was one of the favorite nights for fairies and "wee folk" to be abroad doing mischief. Historically, as well as currently, June has been a time for weddings, as the world is springing into new life. Shakespeare plays with these common beliefs and celebrations in *MSND* with young lovers, weddings, songs, chants, and magic.

Notes on Shakespeare's Language

Generally, Shakespeare wrote in blank verse, which is unrhymed poetry that has a regular rhythm and line length, usually a 10-beat iambic pentameter. In order to determine the number of beats to a line, we "scan" or count them out. Sometimes lines do rhyme, creating a two-line rhymed couplet or a rhymed quatrain. However, not all of Shakespeare's characters speak in iambic pentameter. Often earthy, working-class characters speak in prose. Sometimes magical characters may speak in seven-beat rhythmic patterns, especially if casting spells. The educated members of an Elizabethan audience were aware of these poetic forms and must have enjoyed the heightened meaning as they noticed how different characters spoke. As your students explore Shakespeare's plays, they, too, will begin to notice these variations.

Often when Americans begin speaking Shakespeare's lines out loud, we put on our idea of an upper-class English accent, which is unnecessary on several counts. First, many characters are anything but upper-class. Additionally, the accent of spoken English in Shakespeare's time may be closer to the English still spoken in some pockets of American Appalachia than that which is spoken in England today. Some descendants of those early English settlers never altered their accents or their understanding of Shakespearean vocabulary very much. Many believe that the current standard upper-class English accent (called *received pronunciation*) took hold well after Shakespeare's time. In 1714, German royalty from the House of Hanover became England's monarchs, and wanting to flatter and fit in with their new sovereigns who spoke English with heavy accents, it is likely that the nobility changed their pronunciations to sound more like their foreign rulers. This may be one of the reasons that some pronunciations that we now think of as totally English would not have been the sounds that Shakespeare wrote (Crystal, 2004, 2005a, 2005b; Perkawis, n.d.). An interesting living example of this was shared by an actress friend of one of the authors who recalled that when performing Shakespeare in rural West Virginia in the early 1970s, mothers would cover their children's ears during the bawdy parts of the plays. These same bawdy parts are passages that most of us have to look up to even understand! This demonstrates that the core language and usage from Shakespeare's time is still clearly comprehensible in some communities.

Sometimes, when we scan words for syllables, the additional syllables or missing syllables may be intentional—but sometimes it just may be that the word was pronounced differently when Shakespeare wrote it.

Films Based on *A Midsummer Night's Dream*

There are many film versions of *MSND* that can add to the enjoyment and understanding of the play. The black-and-white 1935 Max Reinhardt production is especially wonderful in its depiction of the mechanicals, who include James Cagney and Joe E. Brown, both familiar faces from scores of later movies. These workingmen have a real bond with each other and enjoy each other's company to the fullest. This film also is amazing for the early special effects with the fairies—effects that were touted in their time (and on the casing of current versions of the film) by *Weekly Variety* (1935) as, "the loveliest, fantastic imagery the screen has yet produced." Sometimes modern students love seeing what was considered amazing to previous generations, especially when it contains ballets with flying fairies.

The more modern 1999 film version, starring Michelle Pfeiffer, Kevin Kline, and Calista Flockhart, highlights the lovers and makes their dramas accessible to student viewers—but be forewarned—the girls are scantily dressed in the forest, and while it is PG-13, this version could cause some blushes. Kevin Kline's Bottom is more poetic and sentimental than most and can lead to a lively discussion about how a role is played.

Sharing films based on Shakespeare's work reminds students of how influential he still is, and also places them in the ongoing company of others who have enjoyed these plays for centuries. You might share clips of both films for students to compare and contrast. Both of these films should be available from local libraries.

AP Classes and Portfolios

Students will undertake an intensive study of this representative piece of Shakespeare's work at high levels of thinking and responding. This book incorporates student research into the historical and social context of the Elizabethan period, which will add layers of meaning to *MSND* and future readings of other Elizabethan plays.

Through close readings and discussions of certain passages, students will use skills of critical analysis, interpretation, and evaluation as they delve deeply into the play. Writing is an integral component of student learning and they will write about the play in varied ways: personal journal responses, essays, research reports, short-answer responses, original poems in meter, creative writing of historical fiction, and analyses of language and structure. Emphasis will be given to helping students express ideas in a clear and coherent manner. Several assignments are appropriate for students to submit for portfolios.

National Standards

As students read, study, perform, discuss, and write about *A Midsummer Night's Dream*, they will gain an understanding of other cultures, make personal connections, communicate their ideas, utilize various comprehension strategies, and appreciate the author's craft. The activities in this book are aligned with language arts standards that are expected of all high school students as they develop literacy skills. Standards are used as established measures to guide instruction. Lessons in this book are aligned to literacy and theater standards and are presented in three tables: Table 1 provides the standards aligning with the Advanced Placement English Literature and Composition course guidelines; Table 2 shows how this book aligns with the National Council of Teachers of English (NCTE) standards for language arts; and Table 3 is based on the standards developed by the American Alliance for Theater and Education. These tables will make it easy for you to see which specific literacy skills of reading, understanding, performing, talking about, and writing about *MSND* are connected to each standard.

By creating, performing, analyzing, and critiquing dramatic performances, students develop a deeper understanding of personal issues and a broader worldview that includes global issues. Because theater in all of its forms reflects and affects life, students should learn about representative dramatic texts and performances and the place of those works and events in history, thus our decision to include the standards laid out in Table 3.

How to Use This Book

Introduction

This section presents general information about Shakespeare, his plays, and a brief overview of *MSND*. It shows you how to use the lessons effectively with students. Included are several brief activities to prepare students to read *MSND*

TABLE 1
Alignment With AP English Literature and Composition Goals/ Curricular Requirements

Goal/Requirement	Reading MSND	Under-standing MSND	Performing MSND	Talking About MSND	Writing About MSND
1. Intensive study of representative works by canonical Western authors from various time periods, engendering careful, deliberative reading and multiple interpretations.	✗	✗	✗	✗	✗
2. Interpretive, textually based analysis that considers a work of literature's structure, styles, and themes.	✗	✗		✗	✗
3. Interpretive, textually based analysis that considers the social and historical values that a work of literature reflects and embodies.	✗	✗	✗	✗	✗
4. Interpretive, textually based analysis that considers a work of literature's use of such elements as figurative language, imagery, symbolism, and tone.	✗	✗		✗	✗
5. Opportunities to develop understanding of a work of literature, enabling students to discover what they think about their reading via informal, exploratory analytical activities.	✗	✗	✗	✗	✗
6. Opportunities to explain a work of literature via expository analyses that utilize textual details to develop and support interpretations of a text's meaning.	✗	✗		✗	✗
7. Opportunities to evaluate a work of literature's artistry and quality, and its social and cultural values, via argumentative analyses that draw upon textual details.	✗	✗		✗	✗
8. Instruction and feedback that help students develop a wide-ranging vocabulary used appropriately and effectively.	✗	✗	✗	✗	✗
9. Instruction and feedback that help students develop a variety of sentence structures, including appropriate use of subordination and coordination, in their writing.					✗
10. Instruction and feedback that help students develop logical, coherent organization in analysis and writing, including specific techniques such as repetition, transitions, and emphasis.	✗	✗		✗	✗
11. Instruction and feedback that help students develop a balance of generalization and specific, illustrative detail in their analysis.	✗	✗	✗	✗	✗
12. Instruction and feedback that help students develop an effective use of rhetoric in writing and analysis, including such features as tone, voice, and appropriate emphasis in diction and syntax.					✗

Note. From College Board (2007).

TABLE 2
Alignment With NCTE Standards for the English Language Arts

Goal/Requirement	Reading MSND	Under-standing MSND	Performing MSND	Talking About MSND	Writing About MSND
1. Students read a wide range of print and nonprint texts to build an understanding of texts, of themselves, and of the cultures of the United States and the world; to acquire new information; to respond to the needs and demands of society and the workplace; and for personal fulfillment. Among these texts are fiction and nonfiction, classics, and contemporary works.	✗	✗	✗	✗	✗
2. Students read a wide range of literature from many periods in many genres to build an understanding of the many dimensions (e.g., philosophical, ethical, aesthetic) of human experience.	✗	✗		✗	✗
3. Students apply a wide range of strategies to comprehend, interpret, evaluate, and appreciate texts. They draw on their prior experience, their interactions with other readers and writers, their knowledge of word meanings and of other texts, their word identification strategies, and their understanding of textual features (e.g., sound-letter correspondence, sentence structure, context, graphics).	✗	✗	✗	✗	✗
4. Students adjust their use of spoken, written, and visual language (e.g., conventions, style, vocabulary) to communicate effectively with a variety of audiences and for different purposes.	✗	✗	✗	✗	✗
5. Students employ a wide range of strategies as they write and use different writing process elements appropriately to communicate with different audiences for a variety of purposes.		✗			✗
6. Students apply knowledge of language structure, language conventions (e.g., spelling and punctuation), media techniques, figurative language, and genre to create, critique, and discuss print and nonprint texts.	✗	✗		✗	✗
7. Students conduct research on issues and interests by generating ideas and questions and by posing problems. They gather, evaluate, and synthesize data from a variety of sources (e.g., print and nonprint texts, artifacts, people) to communicate their discoveries in ways that suit their purpose and audience.	✗	✗			✗
8. Students use a variety of technological and informational resources (e.g., libraries, databases, computer networks, video) to gather and synthesize information and to create and communicate knowledge.	✗	✗		✗	✗

Goal/Requirement	Reading MSND	Under-standing MSND	Performing MSND	Talking About MSND	Writing About MSND
9. Students develop an understanding of and respect for diversity in language use, patterns, and dialects across cultures, ethnic groups, geographic regions, and social roles.	✗	✗	✗	✗	✗
10. Students whose first language is not English make use of their first language to develop competency in the English language arts and to develop understanding of content across the curriculum.	✗	✗	✗	✗	✗
11. Students participate as knowledgeable, reflective, creative, and critical members of a variety of literacy communities.	✗	✗	✗	✗	✗
12. Students use spoken, written, and visual language to accomplish their own purposes (e.g., for learning, enjoyment, persuasion, and the exchange of information).	✗	✗	✗	✗	✗

Note. From NCTE (n.d.).

TABLE 3
Alignment With the National Standards for Theatre Education

Goal/Requirement	Reading MSND	Under-standing MSND	Performing MSND	Talking About MSND	Writing About MSND
1. Script writing through improvising, writing, and refining scripts based on personal experience and heritage, imagination, literature, and history.	✗	✗	✗	✗	✗
2. Acting by developing, communicating, and sustaining characters in improvisations and informal or formal productions.		✗	✗		
3. Designing and producing by conceptualizing and realizing artistic interpretations for informal or formal productions.		✗	✗		
4. Researching by evaluating and synthesizing cultural and historical information to support artistic choices.	✗	✗	✗	✗	
5. Comparing and integrating art forms by analyzing traditional theater, dance, music, visual arts, and new art forms.		✗	✗	✗	
6. Analyzing, critiquing, and constructing meanings from informal and formal theater, film, television, and electronic media productions.	✗	✗	✗	✗	✗
7. Understanding context by analyzing the role of theater, film, television, and electronic media in the past and the present.		✗	✗	✗	

Note. From American Alliance for Theatre and Education (n.d.).

and help students make connections between their own lives and the play's characters. Other activities introduce Shakespeare's language in engaging ways so that students can more fully enjoy the humor and romance of the play.

Use this book as your guide to better understand the play. Through the process of acting, reading, discussing, and writing about scenes, students will notice and appreciate Shakespeare's genius with story structure, luscious language, plays on words, style, and humor. But most of all, enjoy the process of having students immerse themselves in Shakespeare, speak as the Elizabethans did, and add their own individual and humorous perspectives. Share Shakespeare rather than teach it. As Albert Cullum, Laurie's fifth-grade teacher and lifetime mentor said, "Push back the desks" and let the fun begin!

Supplementary Materials

All handouts, quizzes, teacher's answer guides, and activity cards to support student learning, are housed at the end of each chapter.

Chapters 1–5: Reading/Dramatizing the Play Act by Act

There are several activities listed for each act so you can use all or choose the ones that are most appropriate for your class, depending on available time, and the interest, age, or level of learners. The questions and discussion points can assist you in helping students focus on important themes, motifs, language, and structure. The following sections may be included for lessons about each scene:

- **Objectives.** Instructional objectives are included in each lesson that focus on student outcomes.

- **Vocabulary Development.** New words and phrases, particularly those from the Elizabethan period, are highlighted and worked with in various ways in order to help students better understand the dialogue. We find it helpful to discuss the new vocabulary as it arises in the play. However, a few key words could be taught before reading new scenes.

- **Summaries.** At the beginning of each scene is a summary, sometimes broken into sections. Each section represents a time when a particular group of characters are on stage.

- **Best Passages to Dramatize or Read Aloud.** Because there may not be enough class time to read aloud or dramatize the entire play, we have suggested the most salient, interesting, or comedic passages to focus on during class. If this section is not listed, the entire scene is recommended to read aloud.

- **Notes to Teachers.** This presents interesting information or special tips that can enhance the understanding and teaching of the play. From Laurie's many years of acting and directing, we have included helpful teacher tips to enhance the understanding, acting, or directing of *MSND*. These include "From the Director's Chair" and "Production Notes" and will appear from time to time. These notes are boxed separately from the lesson plans in each act for easy reference.
  - **From the Director's Chair.** Notes in this section will enrich understanding of the theatrical aspects of *MSND*. Some will refer to important issues of character relationships, some to technique in playwrighting, while others simply may be odd and amusing.
  - **Production Notes.** These notes will be especially useful to anyone using this book to help with a production of individual scenes or the entire play. If you are planning to produce the play, skim ahead to review all production notes and they will give you a heads-up for all of the preplanning you need to do.

- **Step-by-Step.** A specific sequence of engaging activities is designed to increase the comprehension and clarity of the play. The focus of the steps is noted by the important language arts elements of reading, comprehending, performing, discussing, and writing.

- **Close Reading and Critical Analysis.** Selected passages are emphasized to deepen comprehension of the text and help students appreciate Shakespeare's facility with language.

- **Journal Entries.** Personal reflections to certain passages and prompts encourage students to think, react, and express their ideas in writing. It is an opportunity to ponder, ask questions, make observations about characters or other literary elements, focus on language they like, note passages that are confusing, and make predictions. These may be shared in class and used as a learning tool. The diary entries will help students keep track of the plot, deepen their empathy for the characters, and help them see character development as the play progresses.

Culminating Celebration

This is the final celebration day of *A Midsummer Night's Dream*, which is filled with festivities and merriment. Students will showcase all of the projects that have been developed throughout the study, read their original iambic pentameter poetry, perform their favorite scenes, participate in a "Sweet Talk Challenge," and enjoy sampling the foods of Shakespeare's time.

Introductory Activities

Before we begin the introductory activities, have students organize their binders to help them keep all information together for *A Midsummer Night's Dream*. Tell each student to bring in a three-ring binder and set up individual sections as listed below. If your students cannot afford to buy the binders, you may have them set up similar organizational tools in a folder with brads and pockets, or you can establish a file folder system in your classroom in which students can store their materials. The binder sections we suggest include:

- **Journal.** Journals will be used for personal reflections about characters, plot, and themes stimulated by teacher-selected prompts or self-selected passages. For prompts based on passages of text, you may want students to use the double entry journal format. The lines of text they have chosen are written in the left column and the student response/reflection is written in the right column. They can create this on their notebook paper by drawing a vertical line down the middle.

- **"Words, Words, Words!"** This worksheet, "Words, Words, Words!" (found on p. 17) provides a format for all kinds of learners to keep track of new words and unfamiliar Elizabethan terms. Distribute several sheets to each student to use as needed.

- **Sweet-Talk Challenge.** Students will collect romantic and love-related nouns and adjectives as they read *MSND* so that later they can put them together in the form of "sweet-talk" phrases. As you distribute the three handouts labeled "Sweet-Talk Challenge," do the brief, humorous activity included.

- **Research Materials.** Students will research information on the Internet that relates to the occupations of Elizabethan England. This section of the binder can house all of their notes and writings. If your students do not have access to the Internet, this section can include handouts you have prepared ahead of time or their handwritten notes from research they have conducted outside of class (i.e., in the library, on their home computers).

- **Assessments.** These include evaluation handouts, quizzes, project directions, essays, and rubrics.

- **Notes.** Fill this section with lined paper for note taking in class.

The following activities are designed to increase the students' knowledge base, provide a context, and give them the tools to relate elements of this play to their lives.

Introductory Activities for
A Midsummer Night's Dream

Using the Words, Words, Words! Student Vocabulary Companions

There is a lot of unfamiliar vocabulary in Shakespeare's plays, especially at the beginning. We have found that when students interact with words in an engaging and enjoyable way, they quickly become accustomed to the language and usage. This sheet guides them through learning words quickly, and they may keep track of words for easy reference.

Materials:

- Words, Words, Words! student handout (p. 17)

Step-by-Step

1. Distribute the Words, Words, Words! student handout. Review some key vocabulary words at the beginning of each lesson or words that are noted in your *MSND* text.
2. Engage students with vocabulary words in the following ways:
   - Have students write notes about the words in the given columns on the Words, Words, Words! handout. They can use synonyms or drawings to define the new word in whatever ways are most helpful to them. Students also usually remember the words better when they can associate a word with the name of a classmate who acted it out.
   - To improve comprehension, select key words and have students dramatize them before the whole class or in small groups. You could model an example of "pomp" by walking across the room in a "display of great splendor and magnificence." You would strut across the room with your head held high, shoulders back and straight, smiling at the class as if you had a crown on your head and joy in your heart. Have the class tell what it was in your body language that let them know what "pomp" means.
   - A variation is to list a few key words on the board. Let students secretly select a word, act it out, and have the class guess which word they dramatized.

Name: _____

Date: _____

Words, Words, Words!

A Midsummer Night's Dream Act _____, Scene _____

Word	Synonyms	Word Art/Drawing	Acted/Improvised by

Shakespeare's Language and Style: The Sweet-Talk Challenge

Insult slams employing words from Shakespeare's plays have been enjoyed in many classrooms. Our Sweet-Talk Challenge is an original spin-off of Shakespearean insult slams, but more appropriate to *MSND* with its many expressions of love. Students will find that the various combinations can be hilarious!

Materials:

- Shakespearean Insult Slam student handout (p. 19)
- Collection of Words student handout (p. 20)
- The Elizabethan Sweet-Talk Challenge student handout (p. 21)

Step-by-Step

1. Distribute the Shakespearean Insult Slam handout. Have students choose one word from each column to combine into a fun-loving insult, Elizabethan-style. One example you might give is: "Thou puny, pox-marked ratsbain!" Let them share their favorites.

2. As students read each scene, guide them to find some interesting, descriptive words to list in their journal section. Even if they don't know what some of the words mean, it still gives a powerful and funny effect. Sometimes they can change the usage of the word by making a noun into an adjective, such as "pearl" into "pearly." This exercise also will foster an appreciation of Shakespeare's humor and pungent language.

3. A Sweet-Talk Challenge consists of two or more teams trying to best each other with praise or flattery in the following format:

   "Thou (<u>adjective</u>, <u>adjective</u>, <u>noun</u>)."
   "Thou amiable, orange-tawny pearl."

4. Direct students to start collecting the sweet-talk words on the Collection of Words vocabulary sheet. For example, the second word in the play is *fair*, a great word for future use. At the end of the study of the play, when your students review their entire list, they can pick and choose the "sweetest" combinations. The Sweet-Talk Challenge will take place at the Culminating Celebration.

Shakespearean Insult Slam

Directions: Select a word from each of the three columns and write it on the lines below to create light-hearted Shakespearean insults. Read these aloud with *lots* of expression!

Adjectives	**Adjectives**	**Nouns**
gleeking	fly bitten	canker-blossom
flap-mouthed	urchin-snouted	codpiece
beslubbering	clay-brained	harpie
venomed	knotty-pated	flap-dragon
puking	swag-bellied	lewdster
odiferous	dizzy-eyed	maggot-pie
fusty	toad-spotted	ratsbain
mammering	unmuzzled	strumpet
churlish	reeky	varlot
plumb-plucked	onion-eyed	moldwarp
pox-marked	half-faced	malcontent
tardy-gaited	tickle-brained	scullion

1. Thou _____, _____, _____!
          (adjective)   (adjective)   (noun)

2. Thou _____, _____, _____!
          (adjective)   (adjective)   (noun)

3. Thou _____, _____, _____!
          (adjective)   (adjective)   (noun)

Name: _____ Date: _____

Collection of Words

Directions: As you read *MSND*, keep a list of sweet-talk words to prepare for the Sweet-Talk Challenge at the end.

Adjectives	Nouns

Name: _____   Date: _____

The Elizabethan Sweet-Talk Challenge

Directions: From your completed Collection of Words handout, select your favorite words to make great sweet-talk combinations. You might change the form of the words to make them work. Remember that you want to impress your sweetheart, so pick the absolutely greatest sweet-talk words you can find!

1. Thou _____, _____, _____!
              (adjective)   (adjective)   (noun)

2. Thou _____, _____, _____!
              (adjective)   (adjective)   (noun)

3. Thou _____, _____, _____!
              (adjective)   (adjective)   (noun)

4. Thou _____, _____, _____!
              (adjective)   (adjective)   (noun)

5. Thou _____, _____, _____!
              (adjective)   (adjective)   (noun)

Connecting to Characters: The Roles We Play in Life

When students tap into the emotional conflicts of characters before having to deal with the density of Shakespearean language, they will more easily make connections to their own lives and comprehend the play more fully. After brainstorming various roles they play in real life, students will create modern-day skits that focus on some of the same issues they will soon find in *MSND*.

Materials:

- ❧ Skit Cards (pp. 24–25; copy and cut out these role-play cards to distribute to groups)
- ❧ Teacher's Guide for Skit Cards (pp. 26–27)

Step-by-Step

1. Explain that Shakespeare intended his plays as theater for audiences, not as literature for readers. As discussed previously, he created believable, engaging characters, which are the essence of good theater.

2. Brainstorm with students and write on the board the various roles they play in life. (Include some of the following: student, daughter, son, grandchild, brother, girlfriend, athlete, tennis player, musician, pianist, nephew, friend, boss, employee, babysitter, reader, comedian, volunteer, dog walker, and so forth.)

3. Have students think about how body language and ways of speaking change in different roles. Ask students to give an example of how they might speak to their principal at school, then how they might talk to a buddy at a school dance. Ask students what they noticed (word choice, tone of voice, posture).

4. Tell how the characters in *MSND* also play many roles. Your students soon will meet Hermia, a young woman from Athens, who behaves differently when she is a defiant daughter, a loving sweetheart, or a jealous friend.

5. Teach or review a few key elements of acting that they will use throughout *MSND*. You might bring a couple of students to the front of the class to demonstrate.
   - ❧ *Stance*: Face the audience when speaking so they can hear more clearly.
   - ❧ *Movement*: Use body movements and posture to reflect feelings or emotions. Demonstrate or have a student act out how a character

might show "bored"—slouch in a chair, cross arms, drum fingers on the desk, heavy sighs, and so on. Now, have that person demonstrate "attentive"—sit straight, tilt slightly forward, and look intently at the speaker.

Voice: Show how the way we speak changes in our different roles. Have students give examples of how they might ask a friend to go to the movies together. Now, have them give examples of how they might ask an elderly grandmother to go to the movies. Discuss the difference in words and manner of speaking (e.g., word choice, tone of voice, posture).

6. Distribute the Skit Cards. You should read the Teacher's Guide for Skit Cards before starting this activity. Tell students that they will be creating skits on several themes that are common to teenagers. Have them improvise these everyday scenarios, which are thematically related to *MSND*. Encourage students to use their voices and move their bodies with gestures that express the roles they are playing. This is what good actors do.

7. Give students a few minutes to develop a scenario, and then let each group perform. After each skit is presented, discuss the conflicts and emotions that were present. Each improvised scene is based on a modern-day version of an issue found in *MSND*.

8. After students have performed the skits, you may inform them which part of the play their scene paralleled. This is noted on the Teacher's Guide for Skit Cards. When you come to those scenes, remind them of their skits.

Skit Cards

Teachers: Copy and cut out these role-play cards to distribute to groups of students for their skits. Refer to the Teacher's Guide for Skit Cards sheet to see the parallels to situations in *MSND*. You can remind students of these skits as you read the similar scenes in the play for them to have a stronger emotional connection.

1. A parent refuses permission for his or her child to go to a basketball game with friends at night. Role-play the situation.

2. Two girls are talking about one's former boyfriend who is taking someone else to a dance.

3. Several students are running for school office. Each gives a brief campaign speech, talking about how he or she would be best for the job.

4. A group is in the hall when a student comes up and smashes his locker in anger. He says he is mad because he got a B on a paper instead of an A. After he leaves, the students talk about his overreaction. One of them speculates that he is really upset about his ex-girlfriend going to the prom next week with his current girl-friend's former boyfriend.

5. Two siblings have a problem. One has been given a great gift and the other one really wants it. What happens?

6. A band is preparing to compete for "Battle of the Bands" and planning what songs to play in order to win. Role-play this situation.

7. Two girls are jealous of each other over something. Pick an issue and role-play it.

8. Create a practical joke to play on a friend. Role-play the joke and the friend's reaction.

9. A judge is about to sentence some teens and they plead for leniency. Role-play the conversation.

10. Several of you are singing a song in the talent show. One is the lead singer, the rest are backup singers. Role-play how the lead singer is chosen when everyone wants to be the star.

11. One student was chosen to be captain of the team. Other teammates feel just as worthy and think the choice was unfair. Role-play their conversation.

12. The boy who was taking you to the prom just dumped you. Talk to your friend(s) about how you feel.

13. A couple on a blind date is trying to find something to talk about that they have in common. Finally, they both realize that they like dogs. Role-play this scenario.

14. Your girlfriend went to a game with another guy. She says that they are just friends, she wanted to see the game, and it was no big deal. Improvise your conversation about it.

15. Two groups of students are supporting opposing candidates for class office. Improvise the conversation you might have with a student supporting the other candidate when you are putting up posters for your individual choices.

Teacher's Guide for Skit Cards

Teachers: This sheet gives the connection between the skit and the actual situation in *MSND*.

1. A parent refuses permission for his or her child to go to a basketball game with friends at night. Role-play the situation. (**Egeus refuses to let Hermia marry Lysander and she rebels.**)
2. Two girls are talking about one's former boyfriend who is taking someone else to a dance. (**Helena is upset that her former boyfriend, Demetrius, is now in love with her friend Hermia.**)
3. Several students are running for school office. Each gives a brief campaign speech, talking about how he or she would be best for the job. (**Lysander tries to convince Egeus and Duke Theseus that he is the worthiest young man for Hermia; Bottom tries to convince Quince that he should play all of the parts in their play.**)
4. A group is in the hall when a student comes up and smashes his locker in anger. He says he is mad because he got a B on a paper instead of an A. After he leaves, the students talk about his overreaction. One of them speculates that he is really upset about his ex-girlfriend going to the prom next week with his current girlfriend's former boyfriend. (**Oberon's insistence on getting his wife Titania's Indian pageboy for himself when he might actually be upset because their former loves, Hippolyta and Theseus, are about to get married.**)
5. Two siblings have a problem. One has been given a great gift and the other one really wants it. What happens? (**Rivalry like that between Hermia and Helena or Lysander and Demetrius.**)
6. A band is preparing to compete for "Battle of the Bands" and planning what songs to play in order to win. Role-play this situation. (**Quince, Bottom, and the others try to decide on how to present their play so they will be chosen to perform it for the Duke.**)
7. Two girls are jealous of each other over something. Pick an issue and role-play it. (**Hermia and Helena feud over Lysander and Demetrius.**)
8. Create a practical joke to play on a friend. Role-play the joke and the friend's reaction. (**Puck turns Bottom into a monster when he puts an ass head on him.**)
9. A judge is about to sentence some teens and they plead for leniency. Role-play the conversation. (**Hermia is facing punishment for defying her father.**)
10. Several of you are singing a song in the talent show. One is the lead singer, the rest are backup singers. Role-play how the lead singer is chosen when

everyone wants to be the star. (**Quince tries to cast the play, but Bottom keeps jumping in to try to take all of the good parts. With flattery, Quince manages to convince Bottom to play Pyramus, and only Pyramus.**)

11. One student was chosen to be captain of the team. Other teammates feel just as worthy and think the choice was unfair. Role-play their conversation. (**Lysander when Egeus says Demetrius can marry Hermia; Helena when Demetrius prefers Hermia.**)

12. The boy who was taking you to the prom just dumped you. Talk to your friends about how you feel. (**Helena confides to Hermia about her heart-break over Demetrius.**)

13. A couple on a blind date is trying to find something to talk about that they have in common. Finally, they both realize that they like dogs. Role-play this scenario. (**Hippolyta and Theseus when they are enjoying comparing the sounds of hunting dogs on the morning of their wedding.**)

14. Your girlfriend went to a game with another guy. She says that they are just friends, she wanted to see the game, and it was no big deal. Improvise your conversation about it. (**Oberon and Titania each denying having had affairs.**)

15. Two groups of students are supporting opposing candidates for class office. Improvise a conversation with a student who supports the other candidate when you are putting up posters for your individual choices. (**Puck and First Fairy like each other, but support Oberon and Titania, their masters who are sparring with each other and having a rough time.**)

Connecting to Characters: Elizabethan Hierarchy

Now that students have explored how they play many roles in their own lives, have them explore the motivation of Shakespeare's characters in this activity.

Step-by-Step

1. Tell students that in Elizabethan England the audience came from a tradition in which there was a legitimate pyramid of power with God at the top, then the reigning sovereign, the nobles, and on down to the landowners, craftsmen, actors, and peasants. As Stephen Greenblatt (2004) tells us in *Will in the World,*

> Elizabethan society was intensely, pervasively, visibly hierarchical: men above women, adults above children, the old above the young, the rich above the poor, the wellborn above the vulgar. Woe betide anyone who violated the rules, forgetting to cede place to someone above him or attempting to pass through a door before his betters or thoughtlessly sitting somewhere at church or at a dinner table where he did not belong. (p. 76)

No matter where Shakespeare's plays were set (Greece, Verona, Denmark), the social conventions and political considerations were those of Shakespeare's own Elizabethan England. The class a person was born into affected everything he or she did. Share the following information about class structure in society.

By the Elizabethan Age, some of the rigid class distinctions were becoming permeable.

- Nobility and gentry traditionally were landowners who inherited their wealth and standing. However, one could rise to this class by performing service to the king or queen, studying at the university, marrying well, or slyly purchasing a coat of arms (Greenblatt, 2004; Lace, 1995; Smith, 1967).
- Yeoman, who "derived an annual income of at least 40 shillings from freehold land" (Smith, 1967, p. 153), could rise in society if they acquired wealth through investment or renting to tenant farmers. Artisans and laborers, including actors and playwrights, rarely became part of the elite.

Roles of Elizabethan women: In Shakespeare's England, "most women were deprived of power and authority" and "patriarchal control was the norm" (Rackin, 2005, p. 2). However, Rackin supports the notion that there were many women who did have considerable influence and relative freedom to do as they pleased. The fact that the ruler of England was a woman defied the common view that women were inferior to men. But Shakespeare certainly used the idea of patriarchal control as a plot point in *MSND* with the conflict between Hermia and Egeus, and the Elizabethan audience understood this problem.

2. Give the following prompt, which parallels the situation of Hermia in Act I, scene i: "What do you think about the idea of parents having control of their children's decisions?" Students should choose one of the following three scenarios to write about in their journals (for homework or in class) and discuss their responses:

  You can only date the son or daughter of your parents' friends.

  Your parents have forbidden you to play your favorite sport. Instead, they say you must study _____ (something you detest) for 2 hours every day.

  You've always wanted to grow up to be a _____. Your parents have said you cannot do this and instead will become a _____, and all of your electives must lead toward that goal.

Shakespeare's Language and Style: "Dialogue," (Aside), Soliloquy

Most of Shakespeare's plays contain dialogue, asides, and soliloquies. After this activity, students will be able to identify these when they appear and understand how the style enhances the play.

Step-by-Step

1. Explain the three forms of theatrical address through a demonstration—dialogue, aside, and soliloquy. Do an unrehearsed role-play with a student. Respond to the student's answer to your question, as in the following examples:

   Scenario 1—Demonstrate a dialogue.

   Teacher (to a student in class): Hey, I like your shoes. Are they comfortable?
   Student: Yeah, pretty much (or any answer).
   Teacher: They look comfortable.

   Tell the class that this was an example of *dialogue*, or characters talking back and forth to each other while others in the scene hear what is going on.

   Scenario 2—Repeat the conversation, this time adding an aside.

   Teacher (to the same student): Hey, I like your shoes. Are they comfortable?
   Student: Yeah, pretty much (or any answer).
   Teacher: They look comfortable. (*With hand to mouth, as if whispering something to the class that the student can't hear.*) This kid is so cool, he always looks so relaxed and comfortable.

   Tell the class that this last remark was an example of an *aside*, or when an actor comments to the audience and the other characters on stage do not hear.

Scenario 3—Repeat the conversation, this time giving a soliloquy.

Teacher (to the same student): Hey, I like your shoes. Are they comfortable?
Student: Yeah, pretty much (or any answer).
Teacher: They look comfortable.

> If only I could wear comfortable shoes when I teach—I could be relaxed and "cool!" But no, I have to wear these dressy shoes that hurt my feet and make me really tired. No wonder I'm cranky and feel like I am going to burst into tears. If only my feet were comfortable, how good life would be!

Explain that this last scenario was an example of a *soliloquy*, or a theatrical device that allows a character's innermost thoughts and ideas to be conveyed to an audience without the other characters on stage hearing. In movies, the device of voiceover often is used for this effect.

2. Divide the students into small groups. Have them create their own examples of dialogue, aside, and soliloquy and present these to the class. Discuss.

Shakespeare's Language and Style: Meter and Rhythm

Most of *MSND* is written in iambic pentameter with a few exceptions. We will explore the variations as they appear. This activity guides students toward a rich understanding of this form of poetry.

Materials:

- The **HEART** Beats **OUT I AM** student handout (p. 34)
- Teacher's Guide for The **HEART** Beats **OUT I AM** (p. 35)

Vocabulary

- *iamb*—a unit of rhythm in poetry, consisting of one short or unstressed syllable followed by one long or stressed syllable
- *pentameter*—a line of poetry that is made up of five units of rhythm, for example, five pairs of stressed and unstressed syllables, for a total of 10 beats
- *iambic pentameter*—the most common rhythm in Shakespearean poetry, consisting of five iambs in each line
- *blank verse*—unrhymed poetry that has a regular rhythm and line length, especially iambic pentameter
- *scansion*—analysis of verse according to the rules of meter by scanning or reading carefully the lines for rhythms

Step-by-Step

1. Tell students that in *MSND* characters speak mostly in iambic pentameter (also called blank verse), but they sometimes speak in prose, and in alternate poetic forms.
2. Begin with a word study of *pentameter* and *iambic*:
   - What does the prefix *penta* mean? (five) What are some other words that have the penta prefix? (pentagon—five-sided building, pentathlon—athletic contest that consists of five events for each participant, pentagram—a star-shaped geometric figure with five points)
   - What does the root word *meter* mean? (pattern of rhythm in a line of verse)

- So, what can we infer that *pentameter* means? (a line of verse that has five rhythms, also known as five *feet*)
- *Iamb* means a unit of rhythm in poetry, consisting of one short or unstressed syllable followed by one long or stressed syllable. The adjective form of this word is "iambic."
- *Iambic pentameter* is the rhythmic pattern in a line of poetry that has 10 syllables or five dual beats following the pattern, ba-**BOOM**.

3. To get the cadence of iambic pentameter, have students gently beat their chests in a heartbeat rhythm.
    - Together, say, "ba-**BOOM**, ba-**BOOM**, ba-**BOOM**, ba-**BOOM**, ba-**BOOM**" and then move into saying, "I **AM**, I **AM**, I **AM**, I **AM**, I **AM**" with the hard stress on the "am." This is called an *iamb*. When it is repeated five times, it is called *iambic pentameter*. The five paired beats equal 10 syllables.
    - Explain that this is the primary poetic rhythm that Shakespeare uses throughout his plays. Notice how natural it is, following the rhythm of the human heartbeat.
    - When you see words with accented syllables, such as "armèd," it is read as two syllables, not one. Other words that we would usually consider two syllables, such as "over," Shakespeare may write as one syllable, "o'er," with an apostrophe to shorten it.

4. Read lines from the play and count out the rhythms together. Use the handout, "The **HEART** Beats **OUT** I **AM**." If you prefer, you could make an overhead transparency of the handout.
    - Read the following lines spoken by Theseus and count the beats and syllables. Discuss how each line has five dual beats, equaling 10 syllables. (It is easier to count 10 syllables than five iambs.)
    - This shows how you might count the stressed syllables to emphasize the iambs (although actors would say the line in a more natural way):

        Hip**pol**y*ta*, I *wooed* thee **with** my **sword**
        And **won** thy **love** do*ing* thee **in**ju*ries*,
        But **I** will **wed** thee **in** a**no**ther **key**,
        With **pomp**, with **tri**umph, **and** with **re**vel*ing*. (I, i, 17–20)

5. Tell students that this will help them be aware of the poetic form that Shakespeare uses throughout *MSND*. The variations of this form and other meters used in the play will be taught later.

The **HEART** Beats **OUT I AM**

Context: Oberon wakes Titania after reversing the spell that tricked her.

Directions: Read the following passage from Act IV, scene i aloud. Count the number of syllables in each line and write the number in the space provided. Answer the questions below.

OBERON

	And now I have the boy, I will undo	10
	This hateful imperfection of her eyes.	10
65	And, gentle Puck, take this transformèd scalp	_____
	From off the head of this Athenian swain,	_____
	That he, awaking when the other do,	_____
	May all to Athens back again repair	_____
	And think no more of this night's accidents	_____
70	But as the fierce vexation of a dream.	_____
	But first I will release the Fairy Queen.	_____
	Be as thou wast wont to be.	_____
	See as thou wast wont to see.	_____
	Dian's bud o'er Cupid's flower	_____
75	Hath such force and blessèd power.	_____
	Now, my Titania, wake you, my sweet queen.	_____

TITANIA

	My Oberon, what visions have I seen!	_____
	Methought I was enamored of an ass.	_____

OBERON

	There lies your love.	_____

TITANIA   How came these things to pass? _____

	O, how mine eyes do loathe his visage now!	_____

1. How do the line breaks on lines 79–80 tell the actors to speak?

_____

_____

_____

_____

2. Why do some lines have seven beats?

_____

_____

_____

_____

Teacher's Guide for
The **HEART** Beats **OUT I AM**

OBERON

	And now I have the boy, I will undo	10
	This hateful imperfection of her eyes.	10
65	And, gentle Puck, take this transformèd scalp	10
	From off the head of this Athenian swain	10 (Athenian is 3 beats)
	That he, awaking when the other do,	10
	May all to Athens back again repair	10
	And think no more of this night's accidents	10
70	But as the fierce vexation of a dream.	10
	But first I will release the Fairy Queen.	10
	Be as thou wast wont to be.	7
	See as thou wast wont to see.	7
	Dian's bud o'er Cupid's flower	7 (flower = 1 beat, as in flow'r)
75	Hath such force and blessèd power.	7 (power = 1 beat, as in pow'r)
	Now, my Titania, wake you, my sweet queen.	10

TITANIA

	My Oberon, what visions have I seen!	10
	Methought I was enamored of an ass.	10

OBERON

	There lies your love.	4

TITANIA

	How came these things to pass?	6
	O, how mine eyes do loathe his visage now!	10

1. They tell actors to speak without pause so that the 4 + 6 equals the 10 beat iambic pentameter.

2. Oberon is speaking the magic spell, which is indicated by the seven beats (see p. 6 of Introduction).

Notes: Some lines may seem to read as 11 syllables instead of 10 or 8 syllables instead of 7. However, upon closer study, we can see how the Elizabethans would have pronounced a word with fewer syllables than we might today. For example, in some texts, "flower" is written as "flow'r" and is spoken as one syllable. "Titania" is read as three syllables, as is "Athenian."

Chapter 1
Act I

The course of true love never did run smooth.
—Lysander (I, i, 136)

Act I, Scene i

Objective: Students will read aloud Act I, scene i of *A Midsummer Night's Dream* and discuss the relationships of the main characters.

Materials:

- Character Relationship Chart student handout (p. 45)
- The Three Worlds in *A Midsummer Night's Dream* student handout (p. 46)
- Teacher's Answer Guide for The Three Worlds in *A Midsummer Night's Dream* (p. 47)
- Act I, Scene i Vocabulary Group Assignment sheet (p. 48)

Vocabulary Used Throughout MSND:

- *thee, thou, thy*—you or your
- *hath, hast*—have or has
- *'tis*—it is
- *dar'st*—dare to
- *o'er*—over

Vocabulary in This Scene:

- *apace*—quickly, a fast pace to keep up (l. 2)
- *wanes*—decreases, moves from a full moon to a new moon (l. 4)
- *nimble*—quick and agile (l. 14)
- *mirth*—amusement, pleasure (l. 14)
- *pomp*—display of great splendor (l. 16)
- *reveling*—having great fun and partying (l. 20)
- *vexation*—provoked to irritability or anxiety (l. 23)
- *consent*—permission, agreement (l. 26)
- *feigning*—pretending (l. 32)
- *nosegays*—small bouquets of flowers that are carried, like at a prom or wedding (l. 35)
- *sweetmeats*—candy (l. 35)

- *imprinted*—etched or formed (l. 51)
- *entreat*—plead, beg (l. 60)
- *beseech*—beg (l. 64)
- *abjure*—to give up, to do without (l. 67)
- *barren*—not able to bear children (l. 74)
- *sovereignty*—supreme authority (l. 84)
- *dotes in idolatry*— is head over heels for (l. 111)
- *edict*—a formal proclamation or command (l. 153)
- *dowager*—older woman, often a wealthy widow (l. 159)
- *league*—a distance, about 3 miles (l. 161)
- *steal forth*—sneak away (l. 166)
- *whither*—where, to what place (l. 183)
- *visage*—face or facial expression (l. 215)
- *errs*—makes a mistake or error (l. 236)
- *base and vile*—inferior and worthless (l. 238)
- *waggish*—like a funny or witty person, mischievous (l. 246)
- *perjure*—to lie (l. 247)
- *thither*—toward (l. 257)

Summary of Act I, Scene i

Characters: Theseus, Hippolyta, Philostrate, Egeus, Hermia, Demetrius, Lysander, Helena

Summary: The play begins in the palace of Duke Theseus of Athens where we meet the members of the first of the three worlds of *MSND*—the royal court. Duke Theseus has conquered the Warrior Queen Hippolyta and is going to marry her in 4 days. He wants the festivities to be great and asks Philostrate to see to it. A nobleman, Egeus, enters in a rage at his daughter, Hermia, and demands that the Duke punish her if she refuses to marry Demetrius, the young man Egeus has chosen for her. Hermia refuses because she is in love with Lysander. Egeus accuses Lysander, "With cunning hast thou filched my daughter's heart" (I, i, 37) and he insists that she marry Demetrius or die. Theseus softens the proscribed Athenian law and gives Hermia a choice to marry the man her father chose, become a nun, or die. Theseus and the rest of the court exit, leaving Hermia and Lysander on stage.

Helena pours out her heart

Hermia is upset and Lysander says, "The course of true love never did run smooth" (I, i, 136). But he is a clever fellow and has a plan. They will sneak out of Athens and get married where his rich aunt lives. Hermia is excited about this plan and when her best friend Helena comes in, moaning about how Demetrius doesn't love her anymore (and now loves Hermia), Hermia tells Helena that she and Lysander are going to elope. Then Demetrius will never see Hermia again and be available for Helena. They say goodbye and Helena is left on stage alone.

Helena pours out her heart in a soliloquy, letting us know that she is jealous of her popular friend, Hermia. Helena thinks it is so unfair, "Through Athens I am thought as fair as she. But what of that? Demetrius thinks not so." (I, i, 233–234). Helena decides that she will tell Demetrius that Hermia is running away and gain his company into the woods at night. Now the plot is set in motion with the four Athenian lovers heading for the woods on Midsummer's Eve.

From the Director's Chair: Casting for reading/acting/improvisation throughout *MSND* should be race and gender neutral, with a few exceptions: The lovers should be cast by gender and Thisbe must be played by a male. At the beginning, choose students for main roles who are socially secure and will feel comfortable reading with expression. Encourage other students to take roles as the reading progresses. Different students can read the main roles on different days. Sometimes directors double cast so that the actors playing Titania and Oberon also play Theseus and Hippolyta. This doubling can solve a problem of not having enough actors, but it also can be done to highlight the similarities and differences in the relationships between the two couples.

Note to Teacher: Shakespeare's audience knew where scenes took place because he set it up in the first few lines of a new scene, so stage sets were not necessary. In the classroom, costumes can be fun. Think about simple costume elements that could suggest characters in an uncomplicated way, such as scarves, shawls, sturdy necklaces, belts, strips of fabric, vests, and so on. Collect these washable items and invite students to bring in some, particularly items that they can donate to the class collection.

After the class reads Act I, scene 1, you may want to toss the costumes in the middle of the floor and let students choose a passage to act out and select a costume to suggest their character.

Production Note: If you are going to use costumes when you stage your scenes or production, here is a helpful hint. Because there are so many changing allegiances among the four lovers, it is helpful to color-code them with costumes. For example, you could dress Hermia and Lysander in red, while you put Helena and Demetrius in blue, and it will be a subliminal reminder to your audience of which lovers belong together.

Step-by-Step

Understanding MSND

1. Distribute the Character Relationship Chart handout and read or tell students the story of Act I, scene i (refer to above summary) so that the students can understand the relationships and can follow what is happening. Shakespeare uses dense language, which can be confusing. We don't want students to get

bogged down in the unfamiliar language and lose the engaging thread of the story. The Character Relationship Chart will help to give your students a visual to keep the relationships straight.

2. Distribute the handout The Three Worlds in *A Midsummer Night's Dream*. Choose whether you want to give students a blank version for them to fill out as they discover the characters, or the completed version to help them understand the characters as they go along. If you choose the latter, save the blank one for a quiz. Explain that in this play they will find that all three of these worlds interact.

3. As they read, have students follow along with their Words, Words, Words! sheets (see p. 17). Because the actors/readers cannot use the handout while they read, you can assign a student to be the scribe to record the vocabulary words that the readers can copy later. As students use the vocabulary handout, they can use whichever column(s) helps them remember the words. It's not necessary to have them complete all of the columns. In our classrooms, we found that the "Acted/Improvised By" category served as a trigger for students to remember the words and meanings as they recalled who acted them out. Explain that professional actors must look up these words before performing to understand what they are saying. Back in Shakespeare's time, most of these were ordinary words. Some are unfamiliar because they are obsolete, others because the meanings have changed over time. The *Oxford English Dictionary* and *The Shakespeare Glossary* are great resources for finding the meanings of words used in this time period.

Reading/Performing MSND

4. Read/act out scene i aloud, with different people reading the roles.

Discussing MSND

5. Focus on these discussion points either during or after the reading:
   - **Why does Egeus bring his daughter, Hermia, to Theseus?** (He demands justice from Theseus in punishing his daughter who refuses to marry Demetrius, the man he has chosen for her.)
   - **Shakespeare creates tension throughout scene i. The theme of love out of balance becomes clear right away. What loves are out of balance?** (Hermia is at the apex, with both Lysander and Demetrius in love with her. Helena is on the outside, having been jilted by Demetrius, but she still loves him. Also, Theseus and Hippolyta are somewhat out of balance as we see that he won her in battle.)

Well-loved Lysander

❧ **What emotions are the characters feeling in scene i?** Possible answers include:

- Theseus is energetic and optimistic about his upcoming wedding. He's generous and magnanimous in his softening of the law so that Hermia has a choice and doesn't have to die.
- Hippolyta is subdued about her upcoming wedding. We don't hear much about her yet.
- Egeus is furious at his daughter's disobedience.
- Hermia is defiant, angry, and despairing.
- Lysander is confident that Hermia loves him and is bolstered by her love.

- Helena is jealous of Hermia and devastated that Demetrius doesn't love her anymore and loves her best friend.

6. Optional Vocabulary Activity: Using the Vocabulary Group Assignment handout, have students break into small groups to work through the vocabulary words together by looking up the words in a dictionary or on the computer. Each student should have a sheet, even though students are working together and sharing answers, so he or she will have the worksheet as a reference later. Because some of the language used in Shakespeare's writing is unusual and a bit dense, it is important to spend some time understanding what he is writing. At the beginning of the play, students should learn what some of the Elizabethan words mean, so it will make the rest of the play easier as words are repeated.

Writing About MSND

7. Journal Entry: For homework, have students complete a journal entry with the following prompt:

"The course of true love never did run smooth" (I, i, 136), spoken by Lysander, is one of the most famous quotes from *MSND*. Write a reflection about this quote and how it relates to other literature or movies you've read or seen.

Laurie working with students on **MSND**

Character Relationship Chart
(at the Opening of the Play)

Lysander and Demetrius love Hermia. Hermia loves Lysander.

Lysander   **Hermia**   **Demetrius**

Helena loves Demetrius. Demetrius used to be in love with Helena, but not anymore.

Helena   **Demetrius**

Egeus wants his daughter, Hermia, to marry Demetrius.
He wants Duke Theseus to make her obey him and marry Demetrius, or die.

Egeus   **Duke Theseus**

Date: _____

The Three Worlds in
A Midsummer Night's Dream

Directions: For each of the three worlds in *A Midsummer Night's Dream*, list and describe the characters who live in each in the table below.

Athens Court	Fairy World	Mechanicals
Theseus	Oberon	Bottom
Hippolyta	Titania	Quince
Egeus	Puck (or Robin Goodfellow)	Flute
Hermia	First Fairy, Peaseblossom, Cobweb, Moth, and Mustardseed	Starveling, Snout, and Snug
Lysander		
Helena		
Demetrius		
Philostrate		

Teacher's Answer Guide for The Three Worlds in *A Midsummer Night's Dream*

Athens Court	Fairy World	Mechanicals
Theseus: Duke of Athens	**Oberon:** King of the fairies	**Bottom:** an overly enthusiastic actor who wants to play all of the parts in the play-within-the-play
Hippolyta: Queen of the Amazons (a group of warrior women) soon to marry Theseus	**Titania:** Queen of the fairies	**Quince:** leader of the actors who often is pushed aside by Bottom
Egeus: a nobleman and father of Hermia	**Puck (or Robin Goodfellow):** Oberon's mischievous servant	**Flute:** plays the role of Thisbe in a girlish voice
Hermia: daughter of Egeus, loves Lysander	**First Fairy, Peaseblossom, Cobweb, Moth, and Mustardseed:** Fairies in Titania's train	**Starveling, Snout, and Snug:** members of the troupe
Lysander: a noble youth, loves Hermia		
Helena: friend of Hermia, loves Demetrius		
Demetrius: another noble youth, formerly loved Helena but now loves Hermia		
Philostrate: Master of the Revels, works for Theseus, assigned to plan entertainment for the festival before Theseus' marriage		

Act I, Scene i Vocabulary Group Assignment

Directions: In small groups, work together to find the definitions of the following words, as used in *A Midsummer Night's Dream.*

* Students may improvise short scenes using the starred words if time permits.

Line	Word
14	mirth*
16	pomp*
20	reveling*
23	vexation*
32	feigning
60	entreat*
64	beseech*
67	abjure
84	sovereignty*
153	edict
159	dowager
215	visage
246	waggish
247	perjure*

Act I, Scene ii

Objectives: Students will read, dramatize, and discuss scenes from Act I, scene ii to more fully understand the human experience. Using online sources, students will research occupations that were prevalent in Elizabethan England.

Materials:

- ✀ Act I Word Sort Cards (pp. 55–56; copied, cut, and put into baggies for each group)
- ✀ Quiz on Act I (p. 57)
- ✀ Teacher's Answer Guide to Quiz on Act I (p. 58)
- ✀ Example of a Double Entry Journal student handout (p. 59)
- ✀ Rubric for Journals (p. 60)
- ✀ Occupation Cards for Elizabethan Working Stiffs (pp. 61–62; copied and cut)
- ✀ Rubric for Oral Report and Visual Display (p. 63)

Vocabulary:

- ✀ *condoling*—sympathetic (l. 39)
- ✀ *exempore*—ad lib, without preparation (l. 66)

Summary of Act I, Scene ii

Characters: Peter Quince, Nick Bottom, Francis Flute, Robin Starveling, Tom Snout, Snug

Summary: Six Athenian workmen are gathered in a forest to rehearse a play, in hopes that their play will be chosen to be performed at Theseus's wedding and they'll be richly rewarded. These working men or "mechanicals" all sport interesting names: Flute (a bellows mender), Snout (a tinker), Snug (a joiner), Starveling (a tailor), and Bottom (a weaver). Quince, the leader, describes the play and assigns the parts. Flute is proud of his budding manhood and reluctant to take the girl's part. Quince is constantly interrupted by Bottom, who wants to play every role, "Let me play the lion too. I will roar that it will do any man's heart good to hear me. I will roar that I will make the Duke say 'Let him roar again. Let him roar again!'" (I, ii, 68–71). After the parts are cast, they agree to learn their lines and rehearse the play in the woods the next night.

Note to Teacher: The workingmen of *MSND* are usually referred to as the mechanicals or the rustics. These two terms often are used interchangeably when discussing the characters who form one of the three worlds of *MSND*. A mechanical, when referring to a person, is "engaged in manual labor; belonging to the artisan class" (*Oxford English Dictionary* [*OED*], 1971, p. 1756). Shakespeare used it here and in *Henry IV*. When Puck later refers to them as " . . . rude mechanicals, that work for bread upon Athenian stalls" (III, ii, 9–10), he is acknowledging them as humble workers who earn their livings in booths where they sell their wares or services. Sometimes modern actors and commentators also refer to these characters as craftsmen, artisans, or the rustics. In Shakespeare's era, rustic meant "plain and simple; unsophisticated, having the charm of the country; lacking in elegance, refinement or education; sometimes devoid of good-breeding, clownish, boorish" (*OED*, 1971, p. 2610). Throughout this book we will refer to the workmen as mechanicals.

Note that when the mechanicals are first introduced in Act I, Peter Quince, the group leader, mentions each man's profession as part of his name, a badge of pride and identity: Nick Bottom, the weaver (17) Francis Flute, the bellows-mender (40); Robin Starveling, the tailor (56); Tom Snout, the tinker (58); and the only one lacking a first name, Snug, the joiner (62). Each of these professions has to do with putting things together, making things whole, weaving them together, just as the men are woven into an acting troupe, and woven into the whole of this elegantly structured play. A tinker mends metal household goods, fills the holes in pots and pans, and makes a broken vessel whole. A joiner is not just any carpenter, but the one charged with making things fit in finished woodwork, such as windows and doorframes. A bellows-mender fixes the bellows, a tool with a chamber and flexible sides that expands and compresses to force out air. This device fans the flames to keep the blacksmith's fire hot enough to make metal molten. It is not a stretch to see that each of these skills also are present in the playwright, Shakespeare, who builds plays that are tight and well-woven, and yet breathe with the fullness of a bellows.

Step-by-Step

Understanding MSND

1. Summarize Act I, scene ii before students read the scene, to put it in context and make the reading more understandable.

Reading/Performing MSND

2. Have students act out scene ii. During this time, students should continue filling in their Words, Words, Words! handout. Remind students to look for sweet-talk words to add to their lists.

Mechanicals rehearsing

Discussing MSND

3. Discussion points:
   - **Bottom wants to do everything. How does Bottom try to take over from Quince?** Let students find examples such as the following:
     - Before Quince even has a chance to take charge, Bottom tells him how to take attendance (l. 2).
     - Bottom interrupts to tell Quince how to announce the casting (l. 8).

- Bottom butts in with his opinion and tells the actors what to do, how to sit, and so forth (l. 14).
- Throughout, Bottom tries to usurp Quince's job as director. Quince ends the scene, but Bottom has to have the last word.

What did you notice about how the mechanicals speak in scene ii?
- The mechanicals usually speak in prose, a noticeable difference from the poetic iambic pentameter spoken by the lovers and the court.
- When Bottom is showing off, quoting Hercules in lines 29–36, he speaks in poetry with four beats in each of the eight lines. Shakespearean audiences recognized poetic forms, just like we recognize genres of songs (e.g., hip hop, rap, jazz, rock).
- Some of the verbal mistakes are archaic and funny.
- The mechanicals make bawdy references.

One of the stylistic hallmarks of Shakespeare's writing is what we now might call *cinematic structure*. Because Shakespeare used almost no scenery in his plays, he could move from location to location seamlessly, cutting from a scene in the Court of Athens, to a workers' gathering, to a magical forest glade with no time lapses. Shakespeare changed scenes with a few words of dialogue to inform the audience where and when it took place. Filmmakers use similar editing techniques, ending one scene with a cut, and with a splice of the next film footage, moving to a new location instantly. How far ahead of his time was Will!

Understanding MSND

4. Have students play with vocabulary words through a word sort. Copy several sets of the Act I Word Sort handout, cut out the cards, put sets of cards into baggies, and distribute to groups of students. Let them sort the vocabulary words by matching the words to the correct definitions or synonyms. They may work together to discuss the words, find them in the text, and look them up in a dictionary or on the computer. Many of these words will be used throughout *MSND*, so it will increase their understanding as they learn these words early in the play.
5. If you choose, give the Quiz on Act I.

Writing About MSND

6. Journal assignment for homework or in class: Distribute the Example of a Double Entry Journal handout and explain it. Have students choose a different passage from scenes i or ii, and reflect on it in a double entry journal. They shouldn't summarize, but rather dig into some specific aspect of the play. They could ask questions, make predictions, or comment on language or characters.

7. Introduce the research project on Elizabethan occupations: An Elizabethan Working Stiff.

   ✀ Using the Internet and other resources, students will research various occupations of Elizabethan England. This research project will expand students' understanding of the everyday world that Shakespeare drew on when writing his plays. It has two parts: (1) researching and presenting an oral report with a visual aid, and in a later lesson, (2) writing imaginative vignettes of historical fiction by developing characters based on occupations, much like Shakespeare did.

   ✀ Copy the handout, Occupation Cards for Elizabethan Working Stiffs, cut out the cards, and have them ready to distribute to students in class. Either pass out occupation cards to individuals or have each student randomly pick an occupation from an envelope. (These include all jobs in *MSND*, as well as others.) Direct students to research the occupation they selected.

   ✀ If needed, demonstrate to students how to Google a specific job on the Internet. For example, for "clothier" show how you would search for "clothier Elizabethan England." Either find your own Web sites or go to this excellent site: http://www.elizabethan-era.org.uk/ elizabethan-era-sitemap.htm. If working with younger students, point out the most salient and interesting information about an occupation, such as **made clothes for the nobles and had knowledge of fine and expensive materials.** Guide students to search further about the materials used, what the clothes looked like, and details of their noble clientele. The first site they find may give them links and ideas of where to search next.

8. Have students research their assigned Elizabethan occupations for homework. On a given date, students will make 3–5-minute oral reports supported by visual aids. Distribute the Rubric for Oral Report and Visual Displays to guide their process.

   ✀ *Oral Reports*: The reports could be either factual accounts about the occupations or they could be narratives from the point of view of persons having that job. Either way of presenting is valid, as long as the information is clear and accurate.

- *Visual Displays*: Explain that students will create or bring in a two- or three-dimensional visual aid or symbol to support their occupations. These may include pictures, models, collages, costumes, or other creative materials. This will help students to more clearly understand and remember the occupations and have a stronger connection to them.

Act I Word Sort Cards

Directions to Teacher: Copy and cut out several sets of the words and definitions for students to sort in small groups. You might keep each set of cards in individual envelopes, and distribute the envelopes to small groups for sorting.

apace	quickly, a fast pace to keep up
wane	decreasing, moving from a full moon to a new moon
dowager	older wealthy woman, often a widow
mirth	amusement
pomp	vain display of importance, great splendor
revel	to have great fun; to party
vexation	provoked to irritability or anxiety
consent	permission, agreement
feign	pretend

entreat	plead, beg
abjure	to give up, to do without
visage	face or facial expression
beseech	beg
waggish	like a funny or witty person
perjure	to lie
err	to make a mistake
base	inferior
vile	worthless
edict	a formal proclamation or command
league	a distance, about 3 miles

Quiz on Act I of
A Midsummer Night's Dream

A. Character Matching—Match the character's name to the identification by putting the correct letter on the line.

_____ 1. Egeus	A.	Jilted Helena and now loves Hermia
_____ 2. Theseus	B.	Leader of the mechanicals' play
_____ 3. Helena	C.	Hermia's father
_____ 4. Hermia	D.	Amazon Queen who is getting married in 4 days
_____ 5. Bottom	E.	Master of the Revels, organizes entertainment
_____ 6. Lysander	F.	Loves Hermia, but her father won't let them marry
_____ 7. Demetrius	G.	Duke of Athens
_____ 8. Hippolyta	H.	In love with Demetrius
_____ 9. Philostrate	I.	Loves Lysander
_____ 10. Quince	J.	An actor who wants to play all of the parts

B. Vocabulary—Fill in the blanks with the appropriate vocabulary words that match the appropriate corresponding definitions/synonyms.

visage	entreat	nuptial	waggish	revel
abjure	beguile	wane	vexation	sovereignty

1. _____   to give up, to do without
2. _____   provoked to irritability or anxiety
3. _____   supreme authority
4. _____   relating to marriage or weddings
5. _____   cheat, deceive, or mislead
6. _____   plead, beg
7. _____   have great fun and partying
8. _____   decrease, move from a full to a new moon
9. _____   face or facial expression
10. _____   like a funny or witty person

C. Vocabulary Sentences—Choose five of the above vocabulary words and use each in an original sentence that lets the reader know what it means in context. (Use the back of this sheet of paper.)

Teacher's Answer Guide for Quiz on Act I of
A Midsummer Night's Dream

A. Character Matching

1. C
2. G
3. H
4. I
5. J
6. F
7. A
8. D
9. E
10. B

B. Vocabulary

1. abjure
2. vexation
3. sovereignty
4. nuptial
5. beguile
6. entreat
7. revel
8. wane
9. visage
10. waggish

C. Vocabulary Sentences

Answers will vary.

Example of a Double Entry Journal

Directions: Find a passage you like and write it in the lefthand column. Then think about it; notice the words, language, and meaning and why Shakespeare wrote it this way; and ponder its significance to the scene. Write your ideas about the passage in the righthand column. Ask questions, give opinions, and reflect in this column. This is a place to record your developing thoughts about the play.

Text	Response/Analysis
LYSANDER (I, i, 143–151) Or, if there were a sympathy in choice, War, death, or sickness did lay siege to it, Making it momentary as a sound, Swift as a shadow, short as any dream, Brief as the lightning in the collied night, That, in a spleen, unfolds both heaven and earth, And, ere a man hath power to say "Behold!" The jaws of darkness do devour it up. So quick bright things come to confusion.	I notice that there are four similes in this passage that emphasize the idea that happiness could end at any second for young lovers. It gives me a clear image. There are some "s" alliterations that add rhythm and interest. Personification is here, too, with the "jaws of darkness do devour" phrase, giving night an eerie human quality. I had to read the note to see that there was a play on words on "quick things" and "confusion," because quick means living, not just fast, and confusion means ruin or defeat. So, Lysander is telling Hermia that the deck often is stacked against other lovers, too. As we discussed in class, Shakespeare juxtaposes many contrasting words and images. Here I noticed "lightning" and "collied night" (I had to check the glossary for collied, meaning coal-black), "heaven" and "earth," "darkness" and "bright things." By putting opposites together, it seems to emphasize both contrasting words.

Name: _____   Date: _____

Rubric for Journals on *A Midsummer Night's Dream*

(adapted from "Reading Notes Scoring Guide," 2004)

Directions: Complete all journal entries as assigned. Reflect and respond in a complete, analytical manner that demonstrates your knowledge, insight, and connections. Maintain a neat and organized journal. Include your name and period number on each entry.

Exceptional–A	Commendable–B	Near Proficient–C	Limited–D/F
Completion • all assigned entries • extra effort toward the assignments; thorough • excellent quality of thought, clear connections to self, world, or other texts • neat, well organized	*Completion* • almost all entries • serious effort in writing • good quality of thought with some connections to self, world, or other texts • somewhat neat and organized	*Completion* • most entries • minimal effort given • few connections made to self, world, or other texts • inconsistency in neatness and organization	*Completion* • few entries • little effort shown • no connections made • messy and disorganized • illegible
Content • superb insight; compelling observations and analyses • observations consistently supported by textual evidence • remarks show depth of understanding	*Content* • solid insight, usually precise observations and analyses • observations mostly supported by textual evidence • remarks show basic understanding	*Content* • minimal insight, lack of precise observations and analyses • observations sometimes supported by textual evidence • remarks show some understanding	*Content* • no insight, remarks show no understanding of text • observations rarely supported by textual evidence • remarks are obvious and show little understanding beyond summary

Comments:

Occupation Cards for
Elizabethan Working Stiffs

Note to Teacher: Copy this sheet and cut out the occupations. Be sure to include the first 10.

1 Bellows-Mender	2 Tinker	3 Joiner
4 Carpenter	5 Duke	6 Weaver
7 Globe Theatre Designer	8 Tailor	9 Queen
10 Armor/Sword Maker	11 Hound Breeder	12 Bear-Baiter

13 Actor	14 Poet	15 Tapestry Maker
16 Apothecary	17 Cobbler	18 Lord Chamberlain
19 Innkeeper	20 Midwife	21 Castle Architect
22 Lady's Maid	23 Seamstress	24 Friar
25 Lady in Waiting	26 Miniature Painter	27 Sword Master

Name: _____   Date: _____

Rubric for Oral Report and Visual Display

	4 Exceeds the Standard	3 Meets the Standard	2 Approaches the Standard	1 Does Not Meet the Standard
Content	knowledgeable beyond requirement; thorough with elaboration	good points made but with little variation	information not connected to main idea; skimpy information	irrelevant material that is unconnected to main idea
Organization	logical and well sequenced; easy for audience to follow; flows together well with smooth transitions; display is well designed	mostly logical sequence; somewhat easy to follow; needs better transitions; display is somewhat designed	confused sequence; difficult to follow; lacks clear transitions; display is poorly designed	no apparent logical order; choppy and disjointed; display lacks coherence and design
Visuals and Creativity	materials support the topic in a creative and interesting way	good variety and blending of materials	little variation with limited creativity	insufficient visuals; boring
Elocution	clear voice; well articulated; confident; enthusiastic	clear articulation; varied pace	some mumbling; showed little expression; spoke too slowly or quickly	mumbled; lacked expression
Presentation	engaging; held the audience's attention; poised; eye contact; stayed within time limit; display is highly appealing	held audience's attention most of the time; presented interesting facts; display is somewhat appealing	strayed off topic; presented mostly facts with little imagination; presentation slightly too long or short; display has little appeal	incoherent; no eye contact; failed to hold audience's attention; presentation too long or too short; display lacks appeal; begins with inappropriate remarks, such as his or her lack of preparation

Chapter 2
Act II

Ill met by moonlight . . .
—Oberon (II, i, 62)

Act II, Scene i

Objectives: To more fully appreciate the beauty, relationships, and language of *MSND*, students will dramatize a passage and discuss the effectiveness of the literary elements and devices that Shakespeare uses. Students will extend a discussion by adding relevant information or by asking pertinent questions.

Materials:

- Essay Questions on *A Midsummer Night's Dream* (p. 73)
- Rubric for Essay (p. 74)

Vocabulary:

- *pensioner*—Queen Elizabeth's bodyguard, in splendid uniforms (l. 10)
- *savors*—enjoyment, relish (l. 13)
- *anon*—soon (l. 17)
- *changeling*—in folklore, a child who is swapped for another one by fairies (l. 23)
- *square*—quarrel (l. 31)
- *loffe*—laugh (l. 57)
- *wanton*—carefree; promiscuous; growing luxuriantly (ll. 65, 102)
- *forsooth*—in truth (l. 72)
- *pelting*—insignificant (l. 94)
- *odorous*—fragrant (l. 113)
- *vot'ress*—someone who has taken a vow to serve another (l. 127)
- *chide*—fight, brawl (l. 150)
- *leviathan*—a monstrous sea creature; a whale (l. 180)
- *juice*—nectar from a flower (l. 183)
- *page*—a boy attending on a knight (l. 192)

Summary of Act II, Scene i

Characters: Puck, Fairy, Oberon, Titania, Demetrius, Helena

Summary: Act II begins in the third world of this play, the fairy kingdom, ruled by King Oberon and Queen Titania. Robin Goodfellow, a hobgoblin or "Puck," who is part of Oberon's household, meets up with a fairy who serves Titania and they banter and flirt. They talk about how their masters are mad at each other because Oberon wants a little boy, who is an attendant to Titania. Titania's fairy tries to figure out who she's talking to and asks if he isn't "the naughty Puck." As Robin owns up to his mischief, they are interrupted with the arrival of Oberon and Titania.

Puck and first fairy

Their first lines show their anger with each other, "Ill met by moonlight, proud Titania," to which she replies, "What, jealous, Oberon?" (II, i, 62–63). They express anger and jealousy at each other for past affairs or imagined affairs—including ones with Theseus and Hippolyta. Titania acknowledges that their fights have had a terrible effect on the world and accuses Oberon of having been in a bad mood for months. Because he is so angry all of the time, the fog has made everything soggy, there are floods, crops are failing, sheep are dying, there's no winter, lots of diseases are spreading, and all of the seasons are messed up. She blames all of the evil imbalance of nature on their marital bickering.

Oberon retorts by asking for her page and she refuses, reminding him that the boy's mortal mother who died in childbirth was her friend. Titania leaves with her fairies. When Oberon realizes that he can't get the child by asking, he decides to play a trick on Titania. He remembers that there is a special flower with the power to enchant others, and he sends Puck to fetch the flower. He will use it to make Titania fall in love with some vile creature and give up the boy while she is besotted with love.

While Puck is off fetching the flower, Demetrius runs in followed by Helena pursuing him with love. Although he clearly and repeatedly tells her that he doesn't love her and, in fact is, "sick when I do look on thee" (I, i, 219), she continues to adore him and even begs to be treated like his dog. He runs out with Helena chasing at his heels.

Puck returns with the flower and Oberon gives him the job of anointing the Athenian man's eyes with the magic love juice so that he will fall in love with the young lady who pursues him.

Oberon and Puck

Note to Teacher: From growing up as a country boy in Stratford, Shakespeare was knowledgeable about the plantlife in the natural world. Elizabethan audiences often were familiar with symbolic meanings of flowers.

> *From the Director's Chair:* Although Oberon claims that the source of his gripe with Titania is her Indian pageboy, it likely is that the real source of tension between them is the upcoming marriage of Theseus and Hippolyta and the memories that stirs up for each of them. The Indian boy is probably just a McGuffin. A what? Well, here is a nice bit of theatrical lore. In a movie, play, or book, something that starts or drives the action of the plot but later turns out to be unimportant is called a MacGuffin or McGuffin. The late, great film director Alfred Hitchcock, who specialized in thrillers, coined the term. Hitchcock named the McGuffin, but he obviously didn't invent it. Hundreds of years before Hitchcock, Shakespeare uses the boy as a McGuffin—as we will see as the play progresses. The boy seems important now, but is really just a plot device to get things going!

Suggested Passages to Dramatize or Read Aloud:

- Oberon and Titania, lines 118–150.
- Demetrius and Helena, lines 195–251.

Step-by-Step

Understanding MSND

1. Tell the summary of Act II, scene i.

Reading, Understanding, and Discussing MSND

2. Have students act out scene i or parts of it. Close reading for the following passages is provided on pages 70–71 to help students understand the important scene between Titania and Oberon and the argument that provokes Oberon's trick. Questions that could be asked are listed in boldface.

3. Read aloud the rest of the scene, between Demetrius and Helena, lines 195–251. Discussion points include the following:
   - **Notice some of Helena's character traits.** (She is relentless and keeps coming back at Demetrius. Also, she uses language effectively, with lots of word repetitions. She takes Demetrius' words, twists them, and uses them in a clever way.) Let students find examples and discuss (some can be found in lines 219–220, 235–236, and 244–246).
   - Read line 197, "The one I'll stay; the other stayeth me." Have students discuss this unusual turn of phrase. It's another play on words and contrasts. (Demetrius wants to stop, or "stay" Lysander from

CLOSE READING
Act II, Scene i

TITANIA (ll. 118) And this same progeny of evils comes From our debate, from our dissension; We are their parents and original.	All of the natural disasters she has spoken of happened because the two of them are so powerful and they are fighting.
OBERON (ll. 121–124) Do you amend it, then. It lies in you. Why should Titania cross her Oberon? I do but beg a little changeling boy To be my henchman.	**What is Oberon's assessment of the situation?** He agrees that their fight has caused the natural disasters, but turns it back to her to fix it by giving him what he wants.

TITANIA (ll. 125–142)
 	
               Set your heart at rest:
The Fairyland buys not the child of me.
His mother was a vot'ress of my order,
And in the spicèd Indian air by night
Full often hath she gossiped by my side
And sat with me on Neptune's yellow sands,
Marking th' embarkèd traders on the flood,
When we have laughed to see the sails conceive
And grow big-bellied with the wanton wind;
Which she, with pretty and with swimming gait,
Following (her womb then rich with my young
    squire),
Would imitate and sail upon the land
To fetch me trifles and return again,
As from a voyage, rich with merchandise.
But she, being mortal, of that boy did die,
And for her sake do I rear up her boy,
And for her sake I will not part with him.
	What do you notice about the beats in the line? How is Shakespeare telling the actors to play this section?
	Note that the verse is written in iambic pentameter (10 beats). The "To be my henchman" has five beats and is followed by Titania's reply of five beats to complete the line of iambic pentameter. This tells the actor playing Titania that there can be no pause in her delivery of "Set your heart at rest." She must jump in and continue the meter of Oberon's line. Peter Hall, of England's Royal Shakespeare Company (RSC) is adamant that "the integrity of line structure . . . must be maintained even when a single line of five beats is split between two characters. Particularly then" (Rosenbaum, 2006, p. 232).
	    Titania seems offended by Oberon's request for the boy by her use of the phrase "buys not the child of me."
	    The child's mother not only was Titania's follower, but also her friend. In Titania's fond memory, we see the two of them laughing together, sitting on the beach, watching the merchant ships leave at high tide. Titania joked with her friend that her enormous pregnant belly looked like the full sails of the ships. Just as the ships brought back merchandise to civilization, her friend brought back treats for her.
	    This joyous recollection ends abruptly as Titania remembers that her human friend died in childbirth. Titania's simple final statement shows her grief.
	    What is the effect on the audience when Shakespeare juxtaposes the joyous moments with the tragic?
	The abrupt contrast emphasizes both emotions and makes the words more powerful. It makes audiences recollect how intertwined emotions can be in their own experiences with joy and grief.
	    The language throughout the memory about Titania's dear friend is full of lush, visual images. Shakespeare ends the passage with two stark lines (141–142) to reflect the empty feeling of death.
	    Wherever Shakespeare's plays are set, they are always about Elizabethan England, a place where sea trade flourished. The imagery in this passage reflects the bustling commerce of Elizabethan England.
	    In Elizabethan times the plague visited periodically and audiences were acquainted with the grief that comes with sudden death.

OBERON (l. 143) How long within this wood intend you stay?	He really has no reply to her heartfelt story, so he changes the subject. Notice that compared to how we speak today, Shakespeare reverses the placement of verbs and nouns. **Ask students how they would express Oberon's question to Titania.** (How long do you intend to stay in this wood?) This passage is a clear example of reversal. As you read, your students will find more.
TITANIA (ll. 144–147) Perchance till after Theseus' wedding day. If you will patiently dance in our round And see our moonlight revels, go with us. If not, shun me, and I will spare your haunts.	It is a factual reply, but with an echo back to their earlier jealous argument about their affairs with Theseus and Hippolyta. **How do they negotiate?** Titania offers a barter—I'll play nice if you play nice.
OBERON (l. 148) Give me that boy and I will go with thee.	He barters back: Just give me what I want and I'll go with you.
TITANIA (ll. 149–150) Not for thy fairy kingdom. Fairies, away. We shall chide downright if I longer stay. *Titania and her fairies exit.*	She gets the last word (no way will she give the boy up) and leaves before they argue any more. Note how Shakespeare uses his dialogue to tell actors when to exit a scene, such as "Fairies, away" in line 149.

pursuing Hermia. But Hermia "stays" him, and stops his heart because he loves her so much.)

- **Ask, "Why do you think Shakespeare ended this section between Demetrius and Helena with triple rhymed couplets?"**
  - Helena's final plea to Demetrius is stated forcefully in a rhymed couplet of two complete sentences, lines 248–249: "We cannot fight for love as men may do. / We should be wooed and were not made to woo."
  - But she is not effective and Demetrius exits. In Helena's refusal to accept defeat, she expresses herself dramatically in another rhymed couplet, lines 250–251, which form her theatrical exit lines: "I'll follow thee and make a heaven of hell / To die upon the hand I love so well."
  - Oberon has been watching them and comments on the action with what well could have been a third rhymed couplet, when Elizabethan actors spoke it, lines 252–253: "Fare thee well, nymph. Ere he do leave this grove, / Thou shalt fly him, and he shall seek thy love."
  - These three couplets almost seem like three separate endings to the Helena/Demetrius scene, each couplet seeming to top the last. Perhaps if "grove" and "love" were not a natural rhyme during Elizabethan times, but the actor playing Oberon, spoke them as rhymes, could that have been done to get applause or a laugh

from the word-play loving audience at the Globe? If they were a natural rhyme, could he, as the King of the Fairy World, been declaring his power and right to end the scene? Immediately following these lines we return to the plot as Puck returns with the flower. Shakespeare was a practical theatrical showman writing some of the most popular entertainments of his time. As we note the clever language, as well as the clever plot, it is fun to imagine how the Elizabethan audience may have relished those touches!

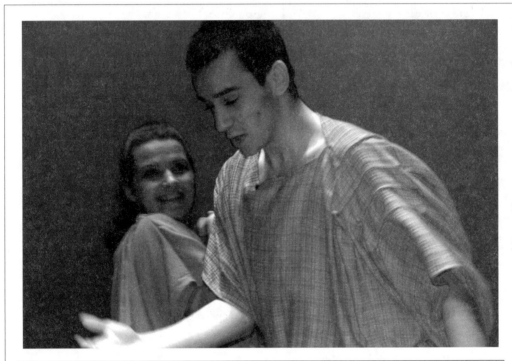

Helena and Demetrius

Writing About MSND

4. Journal assignment: Students should select a passage in scene i and rewrite it in modern language so that it is clear and understandable. If possible, let a few students act out their rewrites during the next class period and compare the language used by Shakespeare with the modern versions that students wrote.

5. Make the essay assignment that will be due at the end of the play and distribute the handouts, Essay Questions on *A Midsummer Night's Dream* and Rubric for Essay. If students select their essay questions early, they can make notes when they find textual evidence to support their topics.

Name: _____   Date: _____

Essay Questions on *A Midsummer Night's Dream*

Directions: Choose one of the following questions and write a focused, well-supported essay in response. Include a brief introduction, at least three body paragraphs, and a substantial closing paragraph. Infuse examples from the text to support your main points. Use the Rubric for Essay as a guide. Be sure to cite the act, scene, and line numbers when using examples from the text.

1. Identify a theme or a passage of more than 10 lines from *MSND* as the source of your essay. If you choose a passage, discuss the poetic form, literary qualities, and meaning. With either a passage or theme (e.g., the significance of magic; how the three worlds work together; jealousy and confusion in love), tell how it is significant to the play and support your thinking through relevant quotations and examples.

2. Dreams are an important theme in *MSND*. Discuss the characters who have dreams, find themselves in dream-like states, or think they have had dreams. Describe the significance of those dreams.

3. Choose a character from *MSND* and present a close examination of the way he or she looks, behaves, speaks, thinks, and feels. Explain how Shakespeare crafted this character to elicit your reaction toward him or her (e.g., sympathy, anger, humor). Give examples of language, interactions with other characters, plot devices, and other character traits to support your thinking. Avoid summarizing the plot.

4. Shakespeare frequently juxtaposes comedic and serious elements throughout *MSND*. Using examples, discuss why he does this and the impact it creates.

5. In *MSND* there are many references to vegetation, flowers, animals, and other aspects of the world of nature. How does this motif weave through the environment of the play adding richness and sensuality in some instances and darkness or danger to others?

Name: _____

Date: _____

Rubric for Essay

Skill Area	5 Responses at This Level	4 Responses at This Level	3 Responses at This Level	2 Responses at This Level	1 Responses at This Level
Content: main idea or thesis of a text; comprehension, insight, and critical analysis of the text.	• in-depth understanding of topic, audience, and purpose; insightful, thorough analysis; clear focus • personal engagement	• accurate, complete understanding of topic, audience, and purpose • clear, explicit analysis in support of the topic	• somewhat basic understanding of the topic, audience, and purpose • partial analysis and explanation	• partly accurate understanding of the topic, audience, and purpose • limited analysis that partially supports the topic	• confused or inaccurate understanding of the topic, audience, and purpose • unclear analysis that fails to support the topic
Development: details and textual examples that develop and support the main idea	• ideas clearly and fully developed, integrating textual evidence • relevant, interesting details with elaboration that supports the main idea	• ideas clearly developed with some integration of examples • most details support the main idea with some elaboration	• some ideas more fully developed than others, using relevant textual examples • some details support the main idea	• ideas partially developed, using some textual evidence but without much elaboration • a mix of relevant and irrelevant information	• some development of ideas, but textual evidence is vague, repetitive, or unjustified • irrelevant and/or inaccurate information
Organization: clear thesis that maintains direction, focus, and coherence; logical order, strong lead and conclusion	• intriguing introduction and compelling thesis • logical and effective sequencing • thoughtful transitions to connect ideas	• strong lead with a clear thesis • logical sequencing • effective transitions	• standard lead with an adequate thesis • ideas inconsistently organized • basic transition words and phrases	• uninteresting lead that fails to focus on a basic thesis • basic structure lacks coherence • few transition words or phrases	• confused thesis, fails to maintain focus • beginning, middle, and end, but lacks coherence • inaccurate transition words and phrases
Language/Voice: precise words to create the intended effect or mood; sentence variety; personality of the writer is evident; natural and compelling	• precise and engaging language with a convincing sense of voice • range of varied sentence patterns that flow with rhythm and cadence	• fluent and original language with awareness of audience and purpose • varied sentence patterns, awareness of different syntactic structures	• appropriate language, with some awareness of audience and purpose • awkward or uneven sentence patterns	• basic vocabulary, with little awareness of audience or purpose • little variation sentence patterns	• imprecise language that is unsuitable for the audience or purpose • some incomplete sentence, no variation in sentence patterns
Conventions: spelling; punctuation; grammar paragraphing; capitalization	• mature control of conventions with no errors	• control of the conventions, occasional errors when using sophisticated language (e.g., punctuation of complex sentences)	• partial control, exhibiting occasional errors that do not hinder comprehension	• emerging control; frequent errors that somewhat hinder comprehension	• lack of control; frequent errors that make comprehension difficult (e.g., use of slang)

Act II, Scene ii

Objectives: Students will explain and advance their opinions by citing textual evidence in class discussion. After studying the structure of the magic spells the fairies cast, students will emulate the format and create their own modern-day spells using seven-syllable lines.

Materials:

- Quiz on Act II of *A Midsummer Night's Dream* (p. 80)
- Teacher's Answer Guide for Quiz on Act II of *A Midsummer Night's Dream* (p. 81)

Vocabulary:

- *pun*—a humorous use of words that involves a word or phrase that has more than one possible meaning

Summary of Act II, Scene ii by Sections

Characters: Titania, First Fairy, Second Fairy, Oberon

Summary of Section 1, lines 1–40: Titania's fairies lull her to sleep with an edgy lullaby of "spotted snakes" and "thorny hedgehogs" (II, ii, 9–10), which reminds us that Shakespeare's fairies have little in common with the stereotypically sweet Disney vision of fairies. Oberon casts a spell to make Titania fall in love with the next creature she sees when she wakes. He hopes that it is a lynx, lion, leopard, or some other vile thing.

Titania sleeps

Characters: Lysander, Hermia

Summary of Section 2, lines 41–71: Lysander and Hermia enter and he acknowledges that he has lost their way and suggests they sleep here until morning. She agrees but insists that he not sleep right next to her. He tries to talk her into being close, but she is determined to be modest. He sleeps away from her.

Character: Puck

Summary of Section 3, lines 72–89: Oberon had told Puck to put the magic potion on the eyes of some man wearing Athenian clothes. So, when he sees Lysander sleeping far from Hermia, he assumes that this is the guy who is so mean that he refused to sleep near the girl. He mistakenly puts the potion in Lysander's eyes.

Characters: Helena, Demetrius, Lysander, Hermia

Summary of Section 4, lines 90 to the end of scene: Demetrius enters once again, chased by Helena, and once again, he refuses to stay and runs off. While lamenting her state, Helena sees Lysander on the ground, and fearing that he's been hurt, wakes him up. Lysander wakes and professes passionate love for Helena under the influence of the spell to love the first creature he sees. Helena doesn't believe this for a second and instead, she thinks Lysander is mocking her. She alternates between chastising him and expressing intense self-pity. Although she does feel real pain, she exaggerates it for dramatic effect, as many teenagers do. Helena exits, followed by the enraptured Lysander. Hermia awakes from a nightmare and discovers that Lysander is gone. She fears for his life and goes off to search for him.

Suggested Passages to Dramatize or Read Aloud:

- ❧ Oberon's speech, lines 33–40
- ❧ Hermia and Lysander, lines 41–71

Note to the Teacher: The song that puts Titania to sleep is spoken in seven-syllable lines. This is a distinct change from the usual iambic pentameter. When otherworldly creatures cast spells, the magic gets focused; the language changes and they speak in seven beats, like an altered state. It's a magical transition time and the rhythms are heightened and compressed.

Step-by-Step

Reading and Understanding MSND

1. Together, read aloud Oberon's brief speech found in Act II, scene ii, lines 33–40. Have the students notice that it is not written in iambic pentameter and make observations about the rhyme and meter. Oberon's speech is made up of seven syllables in each line, and it sounds like an incantation. Discuss the content of his speech and then lead the students into speaking/chanting the short speech together as a whole class or in small groups. Look for this meter to reappear in later scenes and when it does, take note of when and why. Some examples are listed here for you:
   - Puck anoints Lysander (II, ii, 71–89).
   - Oberon talks about the spell (III, ii, 104–123).
   - Puck tells how he will trick the Athenian men (III, ii, 418–421 and 466–470).
   - Oberon undoes the spell on Titania (IV, i, 72–75).
   - Puck, Oberon, and Titania after the spell just as night is ending (IV, i, 97–106).
   - Oberon, Titania, and Puck give blessings to the newlyweds (V, i, 388 to end).

Writing About MSND

2. Homework: Direct students to follow the format of the Act II, scene ii spells: Oberon, lines 33–40, or Puck, lines 84–89. Write spells conjuring up something that they would like to see happen in their own lives. Make sure they use seven syllables per line and rhyme the first two lines and the last two lines. Now the spell is cast! Have a few individuals share some of these spells in class the next day.

Performing and Understanding MSND

3. Dramatize Section 2, the scene where Hermia and Lysander go to sleep, lines 41–71.

> *Production Note:* Note on Staging: After Hermia reclines to go to sleep on one side of the stage, Lysander should come up very close to her. During the lines from 45–70, the humor will be emphasized when Hermia shoos away Lysander, farther and farther and farther, until he is at the opposite side of the playing area.

Discussion points about this scene include:

- **The lovers speak in rhyme and in iambic pentameter. Why do you think Lysander begins with an alternating quatrain poem, in which the four-line stanza rhymes in every other line when almost all of the remainder of the scene is spoken in rhymed couplets?**

  - Perhaps he uses the alternating form because, in spite of trying to reassure his sweetheart, he is, in fact, lost. The alternation of rhyme and no rhyme might reflect his emotional truth of being both self-assured and completely unsure of himself from having gotten lost.

- William Shakespeare is too smart about the battles of the sexes to be unaware of the sexual tensions inherent in a girl and boy alone in the woods at night. The form of the lovers' dialogue is romantic, rhythmic, and reminiscent of a formally structured Elizabethan dance. Lysander repeatedly urges his close presence next to Hermia, which she gently but firmly rebuffs. All of the lines are rhymed couplets, like a predictable dance of courtship, until Hermia finally breaks the rhythm and says, "Lysander riddles very prettily" (II, ii, 59). This is her way of telling Lysander that no matter how much he tries to sweet-talk her into it, she is on to him, and he is *not* going to be sleeping next to her.

- Right before the end of their scene when Hermia and Lysander are far across the stage from each other, they make vows to stay true until death. **Ask students to predict whether these vows will hold.** (You might comment to students when they predict that the vows will be broken that they are using their accumulated knowledge of storytelling and playwriting.) Although there is no evidence from the characters of Lysander and Hermia to predict trouble, conflict must be coming or Shakespeare wouldn't have bothered to include this scene.

- Have students notice the word repetitions, plays on words, and puns and discuss how effectively Shakespeare uses these devices. Repetition of words and phrases is a writing craft often used by writers to emphasize something important or to give impact and increased attention to the word or phrase. It also can be playful, like the repetitions of words or lines in nursery rhymes and songs. In just one conversation between Lysander and Hermia, observe how many repetitions are present. Students can find even more throughout the play. Just make them aware of this technique and the reasons for this emphasis so that they can observe other instances. The repetitions in this scene include:

  - **one** turf, **one** heart, **one** bed, **one** troth, **one** heart (II, ii, 47–48, 54)

- **Lie** further off, **lie** so near, for **lying** so, I do not **lie**, Lysander **lied**, **lie** further off (II, ii, 50, 58, 61, 63) In addition to the repetitions, *lie* also becomes a pun.
- my **heart** unto yours is knit, one **heart** we can make (II, ii, 53–54)
- Fair **love**, **Love** takes the meaning of **love's** conference, for **love** and courtesy, Thy **love** ne'er alter (II, ii, 41, 52, 62, 67)

4. Tell the summary for Section 3, lines 72–89. Point out to students that once again, we hear the magical incantation of seven syllables.
5. Tell the summary for Section 4, lines 90 to the end of the scene.
6. Read/act out lines 90 to the end of the scene. Direct students to turn and talk to one person about the feelings of the lovers after the magical love juice, then share ideas.

Writing About MSND

7. Journal entry: Have students write a diary entry from the perspective of Demetrius, Lysander, Hermia, or Helena about the night in the forest, answering the prompt, "How did I feel about what happened tonight and what do I want?" Shakespeare wrote for the theater and effective actors need to know their character's objective, their "what do I want?" This prompt will help students think like actors, which is a valuable skill in reading plays.
8. Give the quiz as a take-home assignment for Act II.

Name: _____   Date: _____

Quiz on Act II of
A Midsummer Night's Dream

A. Character Identification—Tell who each character is.

1. Robin Goodfellow _____

2. Oberon _____

3. Titania _____

B. Vocabulary—Fill in the blanks with the appropriate vocabulary words that match the corresponding definitions/synonyms.

pensioner   chide   savor   anon   sprite   forsooth   odorous   cross   leviathan   page

1. _____   in truth, certainly

2. _____   a monstrous sea creature; whale

3. _____   bodyguard who serves the queen, wears splendid uniforms

4. _____   soon

5. _____   boy attending on a knight

6. _____   to fight or brawl

7. _____   spirit

8. _____   enjoyment and relish

9. _____   fragrant

10. _____   oppose, resist

C. Short Answer—Answer the following questions:

1. Why won't Titania give the boy to Oberon?

_____

_____

2. Why does Puck put the flower juice on Lysander's eyes?

_____

_____

3. How does Helena react to Lysander's profession of love?

_____

_____

4. In this act, what does the use of meter tell us about Puck? About Hermia?

_____

_____

Advanced Placement Classroom: A Midsummer Night's Dream © Prufrock Press • This page may be photocopied or reproduced with permission for classroom use.

Teacher's Answer Guide for
Quiz on Act II of
A Midsummer Night's Dream

A. Character Identification

1. Also known as Puck; a mischievous sprite or hobgoblin; in Oberon's service
2. King of the Fairies
3. Queen of the Fairies

B. Vocabulary

1. forsooth
2. leviathan
3. pensioner
4. anon
5. page
6. chide
7. sprite
8. savor
9. odorous
10. cross

C. Short Answer

1. She feels an allegiance to her friend, the boy's mother, and wants to raise him herself.
2. He makes a mistake. When he sees a young man dressed in Athenian clothing sleeping in the forest, he erroneously assumes it is Demetrius.
3. She doesn't believe him and is infuriated that he is poking fun at her.
4. The seven-beat meter tells us that Puck holds the power of magic. We have seen that magic spells are performed in a seven-beat meter. Hermia speaks in iambic pentameter, which is used by the upper-class characters. It is poetic and lyrical and fits the speech of the lovers.

Chapter 3
Act III

Out of this wood do not desire to go.
Thou shalt remain here, whether thou wilt or no.
—Titania (III, i, 154–155)

Act III, Scene i

Objectives: During a close reading, students will critically analyze a section of the play, explain, and defend their interpretations. Students will present their research on Elizabethan occupations in an oral report supported by a visual aid. Students will produce a well-developed, clearly written piece of historical fiction that utilizes effective language and voice appropriate for the purpose.

Materials:

- Checklist for Writing Historical Fiction (p. 91)

Vocabulary:

- *parlous*—perilous or uncertain (l. 13)

- *prologue*—an introduction that goes before a play or novel (l. 17)

- *casement*—a window that opens on hinges instead of sliding up and down (l. 55)

- *cue*—a line or action that prompts an actor to say his next line (l. 75)

- *odious*—hateful, disgusting (l. 81)

- *knavery*—dishonest or deceitful behavior (l. 122)

- *gleek*—to jest, to make a joke (l. 148)

Production Notes: As you help your students perform these scenes, you will discover, as every other actor or director doing these scenes in the last 400 years has, that almost every mention of the word *ass* gets a laugh. Your actors will have to hold for the laugh, which means to pause and let the audience enjoy the joke before speaking the next line. Otherwise the audience will miss the next line. These laughs will build until the climax with Puck's great couplet, "When in that moment, so it came to pass, Titania waked and straightway loved an ass" (III, ii, 35–36). Shakespeare wrote for every member of his audience!

Summary of Act III, Scene i

Characters: Titania, Bottom, Quince, Snout, Starveling, Puck, Flute, Peaseblossom, Cobweb, Moth (sometimes called Mote), Mustardseed

Summary: The mechanicals rehearse their play, making many mistakes. Puck plays a trick on Bottom, transforming him into a man with the head of an ass. After his friends run away in fear, he sings and Titania awakes and (due to the spell) is enraptured. She proclaims her love and her power and calls her fairies to attend on him and bring him treats. They all exit.

Step-by-Step

1. Your students should have their reports on Elizabethan occupations (see p. 53) ready at this point. Before the oral reports begin, direct the students to listen carefully to the reports on various occupations. Tell students that after the presentations they will choose a different occupation from the one they have reported on and then create a piece of historical fiction on their new job. This assignment requires students to imagine a change in focus from their original occupation to something else.

2. Have students present their oral reports with props on their Elizabethan Working Stiff.

3. Tell students that each scenario is unique and requires that they will:
   - listen closely to a fellow student's oral report in order to learn about that career, and
   - gather enough information from the oral reports to respond in the next assignment. They should *not* use other research; just their classmates' shared knowledge.

4. When students have collected the information, instruct them to write a 1–2-page piece of historical fiction. Distribute the handout, Checklist for Historical Fiction Writing. This might be written as a first person diary entry, or as a third person story, or even using dialogue in a short play. For this assignment, no outside research is allowed, just close listening to their classmates who presented the Elizabethan occupations in their oral reports. If time permits, some of these can be read aloud in class and should be included in the Culminating Celebration. Examples are included in Figure 1.

5. Remind students that they have learned much about various Elizabethan occupations through this lesson. Shakespeare drew on a broad range of knowledge of varied occupations in his writing. He wrote about people from many parts of the social order in Elizabethan England, including monarchs and nobility, as well as barmaids and jesters. In *A Midsummer Night's Dream* many of these characters from different stations in life are pulled together.

> **Example for "Tinker"**
> **(First person perspective)**
>
> Tinkering had been a fine life, but after that amazing dream, I realized that I had to stop traveling and settle down. I had my eye on the cobbler's wife, since the cobbler had run off to sea. Here is the story of how I became a cobbler to the queen. . . .
>
> **Example for "Seamstress"**
> **(Third person perspective)**
>
> Working as a seamstress may have "seamed" like a good idea to her mother when she sent Charlotte off to learn the trade. But the girl knew that she was worthy of better things. She saw no reason why she couldn't become a lady's maid and live in a fine manor instead of working in that hovel. No more pricked fingers for her! All Charlotte had to do was . . .
>
> ――――――――――――――――――――――――――――――――――――――
>
> *Figure 1.* Examples of historical fiction on Elizabethan occupations

From the Director's Chair: When the mechanicals begin to rehearse their play, like anyone in commercial show business, they consider their audience and make adjustments to their script so that they won't frighten or offend their patrons and their audience. Once again, Shakespeare is granting us a sly glimpse of what must have happened frequently in his own troupe. Flattery to Queen Elizabeth was always allowed, but anything that could have been taken critically had to be scrutinized with care.

We see the actors make common mistakes that occur in rehearsals: mispronouncing an unfamiliar name in the script and missing or confusing a cue. Are they meeting at Ninus's Tomb or Ninny's Tomb? Are the flowers odious or odorous? Frustration mounts as Quince tries to direct his actors who can't seem to get cues, lines, blocking, or anything else right. This is the sort of scene that all audiences love, but especially theatrical ones! Explain and discuss these ties to theatre with your students before they read Act III, scene i.

Reading and Understanding MSND

6. Read the summary of scene i to the students and discuss lines 1–126 that involve Bottom, Quince, Snug, Flute, Snout, Starveling, and Puck. Discussion points for this section include:

    ❧ Why do you think Shakespeare included this 4-page scene here, considering that only the last page of this scene is integral to the plot?

- Shakespeare was an actor as well as a playwright who was part of the company, and once again with great affection, he shows the process of producing a play.
- In Act I, we saw the troupe casting the play. Now, we come to the next step: the script conference about the problems in the play, such as staging issues (with the wall and moon) and rehearsing lines (including where they get words wrong, such as odious/ odorous).

From the Director's Chair: Frequently, the mechanicals mistake words in ludicrous ways and this sort of mistaken usage is now called a *malaprop*. Shakespeare created his malapropisms for the mechanicals in *MSND* long before they were called this. For those who love the theatrical origins of wonderful words in our English language, here is a fun one. Calling this type of a mistake a malaprop originated with the character Mrs. Malaprop in the play *The Rivals*, written in 1775 by Richard Sheridan. Mrs. Malaprop misused words with great abandon and was probably named based on the French phrase *mal a propos*, meaning inappropriate. One can wonder, was Sheridan thinking of Shakespeare's Bottom when he created Mrs. Malaprop, whose name now describes the mechanicals? The affectionate tributes from artist to artist never stop!

- **Have the students find the mechanicals' malapropisms** (using wrong but similar words unintentionally), which Shakespeare included for comic effect. After they find some, ask if they can think of other characters who display this trait (such as Amelia Bedelia and Archie Bunker). Some malaprops they may find include:
  - *disfigure*: should be "figure," which means "represent" (line 59)
  - *odious*: Quince corrects Bottom, and tells him that the word should be "odors," which means "a smell," whether pleasant or unpleasant. Odious means "hateful." This one is a double malaprop, because the correction to "odors" from "odious" is still wrong! Quince should have told Bottom to say, "odorous!" (line 81)
  - *he goes but to see a noise*: Quince gives us this malaprop, which should be "hear a noise" (line 90)
  - *translated*: Quince means to say "transformed" (line 120)

- Although the mechanicals are not formally educated by Elizabethan standards, it is worthwhile to note that as artisans creating theater, they share a skill that even a slightly educated Elizabethan audience might have shared—a basic appreciation of poetic forms. When

Quince is trying to assert his leadership and choose the best form for the newly added prologue, he suggests that it be "written in eight and six" (24). Bottom, who wants something other than the standard ballad meter, counters, "No, make it two more. Let it be written in eight and eight." (25–26)

Titania snuggles with Bottom

7. Do a close reading and analysis of lines 121–208 with Titania and Bottom, using the close reading on the following page as a guide. Remind students that they may find many sweet-talk words to add to their lists.

Performing MSND

8. After the close reading and studying of this passage, have students act it out.

Writing About MSND

9. Journal Entry: Have students select a few lines that resonate with them. Write these lines and a reflection in a double entry journal (see p. 59 for an example).

CLOSE READING
Bottom and Titania's Meeting in Act III, Scene i

BOTTOM (Lines 127–130) (*He sings.*) *The ouzel cock, so black of hue,* *With orange-tawny bill,* *The throstle with his note so true,* *The wren with little quill—*	Bottom is not a great singer but he is singing to reassure himself when he finds he is alone in the woods and his friends have run away from him in fear. (Singing to counter fear is a much-used human and theatrical device.) You might direct whoever is reading Bottom's part to sing off-key. Notice Shakespeare's focus on nature again, which is a motif that runs throughout this play and this section.
TITANIA (Line 131) (*waking up*) What angel wakes me from my flow'ry bed?	This is the first time that characters from the two worlds converse. Because of Oberon's spell, Titania wakes and sees this misshapen ass-headed workingman as an alluring creature.
BOTTOM (Lines 132–138) (*sings*) *The finch, the sparrow, and the lark,* *The plainsong cuckoo gray,* *Whose note full many a man doth mark* *And dares not answer "nay"—* for, indeed, who would set his wit to so foolish a bird? Who would give a bird the lie though he cry "cuckoo" never so?	Bottom continues his song and philosophizes about the nature of birds. Although he is a humorous character, he does think about things deeply (perhaps bottomlessly).
TITANIA (Lines 139–143) I pray thee, gentle mortal, sing again. Mine ear is much enamored of thy note, So is mine eye enthrallèd to thy shape, And thy fair virtue's force perforce doth move me On the first view to say, to swear, I love thee.	As Titania addresses Bottom for the first time, her vocabulary is exaggerated, almost ecstatic, using words of love, such as *enamored*, *enthralled*, and *moved me*. She arrests herself when the word *say* is not strong enough, and exchanges it for the more passionate *swear*. "On the first view, to *say*, to *swear*, I love thee" (l. 143, italics added). This repetition enlarges, exaggerates, and underscores her emotions.
BOTTOM (Lines 144–149) Methinks, mistress, you should have little reason for that. And yet, to say the truth, reason and love keep little company together nowadays. The more the pity that some honest neighbors will not make them friends. Nay, I can gleek upon occasion.	Bottom's common sense insight into love, that romantic passion and good sense don't usually go together, is in enormous contrast to Titania's declaring her passion to a stranger.
TITANIA (Line 150) Thou art as wise as thou art beautiful. BOTTOM (Lines 151–153) Not so neither; but if I had wit enough to get out of this wood, I have enough to serve mine own turn.	Bottom doesn't jump at the flattery. Instead, he tells the simple truth—that he'd like to get out of the woods. **Do you think that Bottom is wise? In what ways is he wise? In what ways is he foolish?** He is wise in that he understands that romance and common sense don't always go together, and that flattery isn't going to sidetrack him. He is knowledgeable about many subjects. He seems foolish that he is ignoring this beautiful fairy who is doting on him.
TITANIA (Lines 154–164) Out of this wood do not desire to go. Thou shalt remain here whether thou wilt or no. I am a spirit of no common rate. The summer still doth tend upon my state, And I do love thee. Therefore go with me. I'll give thee fairies to attend on thee, And they shall fetch thee jewels from the deep And sing while thou on pressèd flowers dost sleep. And I will purge thy mortal grossness so That thou shalt like an airy spirit go.— Peaseblossom, Cobweb, Mote, and Mustardseed! (*The fairies enter, lines 165–169*)	No matter what he wants, he will stay as long as she wants him because she is powerful. She promises to treat him extravagantly and to magically transform him from an earthbound creature into one who can fly. Note the double meaning of the word *purge*, which means, "transform him" but also could mean to cause a bowel movement. An Elizabethan audience would have known both meanings, and the play on words would have gotten a laugh from the nobility, as well as the workers. Notice the "s" alliteration. It seems whispery, soft, and seductive.

TITANIA (Lines 170–180) Be kind and courteous to this gentleman. Hop in his walks and gambol in his eyes; Feed him with apricocks and dewberries, With purple grapes, green figs, and mulberries; The honey-bags steal from the humble-bees, And for night-tapers crop their waxen thighs And light them at the fiery glowworms' eyes To have my love to bed and to arise; And pluck the wings from painted butterflies To fan the moonbeams from his sleeping eyes. Nod to him, elves, and do him courtesies. (*The fairies greet Bottom lines 181–184*)	She summons the fairies to wait upon him, and directs them to bring him delicacies, even if it takes violence to do so. Notice *steal* the honey bags, *crop* waxen thighs, and *pluck* the wings. ***Note to Teacher***: Titania is trying to seduce Bottom and this passage is filled with sexual innuendo that you may or may not want to discuss with students. For example, when she says, "To have my love to bed and to arise," she is probably talking about sexual arousal. Some students may pick up on this themselves and comment in class. We often discuss with our students that Shakespeare was rather bawdy and the Elizabethan audience was not squeamish about these allusions to sexual behavior.
BOTTOM (Lines 185–203) I cry your Worships mercy, heartily.—I beseech your Worship's name. **COBWEB** Cobweb. **BOTTOM** I shall desire you of more acquaintance, good Master Cobweb. If I cut my finger, I shall make bold with you.—Your name, honest gentleman? **PEASEBLOSSOM** Peaseblossom. **BOTTOM** (Lines 192–203) I pray you, commend me to Mistress Squash, your mother, and to Master Peascod, your father. Good Master Peaseblossom, I shall desire you of more acquaintance, too.—Your name, I beseech you, sir? **MUSTARDSEED** Mustardseed. **BOTTOM** Good Master Mustardseed, I know your patience well. That same cowardly, giantlike ox-beef hath devoured many a gentleman of your house. I promise you, your kindred hath made my eyes water ere now. I desire you of more acquaintance, good Master Mustardseed.	Bottom doesn't seem to show any interest in Titania. Bottom banters with the fairies, finding something in each name to comment on, using his quick wit. (Cobweb as a bandage, Peaseblossom and the vegetable parentage, and Mustardseed makes his eyes water.)

TITANIA (Lines 204–208)
Come, wait upon him. Lead him to my bower.
  The moon, methinks, looks with a wat'ry eye,
And when she weeps, weeps every little flower,
  Lamenting some enforcèd chastity.
Tie up my lover's tongue. Bring him silently.
	She shows impatience. She wants to get her new lover back to her private enclosure. Is she jealous that he's bantering with the fairies?
	
	    She tells the fairies to stop talking, shut him up, and bring him to her.
	
	    What do you notice about the way both characters speak?
	
	    Titania speaks in iambic pentameter and Bottom speaks in prose.
	
	    Notice that both the content and the form of speech express the character. Titania's elevated, flowery language flows in the poetic meter of iambic pentameter. Bottom's ordinary prose and basic concerns for food and rest fit with his position as a working man in Athens.

Checklist for Writing Historical Fiction

Have I . . .

❏ justified the character's transition from one occupation to a new one?

❏ developed the character by giving details of the way the character looks, acts, speaks, and thinks or feels?

❏ created an interesting plot?

❏ used an authentic voice throughout the piece?

❏ showed knowledge of the character's two occupations by including facts and information?

Act III, Scene ii

Objective: To enhance comprehension, students will create tableaus of various scenarios and explain the importance of each one.

Materials:

- Tableau Cards for the Fight Scene (p. 100; copy, cut, and distribute to students)
- Quiz on Act III of *A Midsummer Night's Dream* (p. 101)
- Teacher's Answer Guide for Quiz on Act III of *A Midsummer Night's Dream* (p. 102)

Vocabulary:

- *counterfeit*—phony (l. 303)
- *personage*—grand or important stature (l. 307)
- *maypole*—tall and skinny pole used in May Day celebrations, usually decorated with ribbons and flowers (l. 311)
- *shrewd*—quarrelsome, argumentative (l. 340)
- *vixen*—a woman who is malicious with a fierce temper (l. 341)
- *fray*—a rough and tumble fight (l. 363)
- *'nointed*—(anointed)—rubbed ointment on a part of someone's body (l. 372)

Summary of Act III, Scene ii by Sections:

Break up the reading/dramatizing of this scene into the following six sections.

Characters: Oberon, Puck

Summary of Section 1, lines 1–44: Puck enters and with great glee tells Oberon that Titania is in love with a monster. He relates that the working men from Athens, "A crew of patches, rude mechanicals" (III, ii, 9), were rehearsing their play and he decided to play a trick on the simpletons, the humble workers, and put an ass head on one of them. Bottom (transformed with the ass head) awakens Titania, leading to this great couplet: "When in that moment, so it came to pass, Titania waked and straightway loved an ass" (III, ii, 35–36). Demetrius and Hermia enter and Puck proclaims that this is not the man he enchanted at Oberon's earlier request.

Characters: Demetrius, Hermia

Summary of Section 2, lines 45–89: When we last saw Hermia, she had awakened and found Lysander gone. Now she enters with Demetrius and thinks that he must have hurt Lysander. She demands that Demetrius tell her where Lysander is, but because he knows nothing, he can't tell her anything. She tries to cajole the answer from him and then berates him for not telling her anything. She storms out. He realizes that he is very tired in his sorrow over Hermia's rejection, so he decides to go to sleep.

Characters: Oberon, Puck, Demetrius

Summary of Section 3, lines 90–123: Oberon and Puck were watching Hermia and Demetrius, and now Oberon blames Puck for putting the love juice on the wrong lover's eyes. He sends Puck to find Helena and he anoints Demetrius's sleeping eyes with the magic flower. Puck returns, telling Oberon that Helena and Lysander are approaching and points out, "Lord, what fools these mortals be!" (III, ii, 117). Oberon and Puck step aside, magically invisible to the approaching mortals.

Characters: Lysander, Helena, Demetrius, Hermia

Summary of Section 4, lines 124–365: Lysander proclaims his love to Helena as they enter. She tells him to stop mocking her because she knows that he really loves Hermia. Demetrius wakes up, sees Helena, and raves that she is " . . . goddess, nymph, perfect, divine!" (III, ii, 140). She gets angry, thinking that they are both making fun of her and chides them for their behavior. Each suitor protests that he is true and the other one really loves Hermia. Then Hermia enters, happy that she has found her Lysander but confused when he says that he now loves Helena. Helena is convinced that Hermia is part of their confederacy to mock her and appeals to their long-time friendship. Hermia is amazed, because from her point of view, Helena has stolen the love of Lysander. All of the old envies within the girls' friendship with each other come out including Helena being taller and Hermia being shrewish. The two girls square off in anger with the boys trying to intervene. The boys dare each other to fight for Helena's love and they exit. Helena doesn't trust Hermia's anger and runs away. Hermia also exits.

Hermia is not pleased

Demetrius and Lysander square off

Characters: Oberon, Puck

Summary of Section 5, lines 366–421: Puck defends himself for mistaking the Athenian boys and reminds Oberon, "Did not you tell me I should know the man / By the Athenian garments he had on?" (III, ii, 369–370). Oberon sends Puck off to distract and confuse Lysander and Demetrius so that they cannot fight and gives Puck another magic flower to remove the enchantment from Lysander. Oberon says he will convince Titania to give up her boy and undo his spell on her. Puck reminds Oberon that it is almost morning when ghosts of damned people must return to their miserable graves. Oberon points out that he is a different sort of spirit and loves the daylight.

Characters: Puck, Lysander, Demetrius, Helena, Hermia

Summary of Section 6, lines 422–end: Lysander and Demetrius run in and out, making bellicose threats but missing each other as Puck leads them astray by calling out in the voice of one or the other. Eventually each of the lovers enters and falls asleep in despair. After they are all asleep, Puck undoes the charm and promises that when Lysander wakes, "Thou tak'st / True delight / In the sight / Of thy former lady's eye" (III, ii, 483–486).

Suggested Lines to Dramatize:

- Lysander, Demetrius, Helena, and Hermia, lines 258–365

Production Notes: There are many opportunities to enhance the textual humor with physical humor if time and skill permit. From line 264 until Lysander and Demetrius leave, there should be quite a bit of jockeying and position changing. First Hermia holds onto Lysander (line 265) who later has to keep Hermia from attacking Helena. Some "bits" that can work if the sizes of your actors can accommodate them and if they are well rehearsed might include:

- Hermia holding onto Lysander and changing hands as she circles him to get and keep his attention.

- Hermia jumping on Lysander's back so that when he says, "Hang off, thou cat, thou burr! Vile thing, let loose, Or I will shake thee from me like a serpent (270–271). Lysander can try to shake her off and she can adjust and readjust her hold, and then answer sweetly in her next line.

- Another bit of physical comedy could be to have Hermia make a running leap at Helena but be caught by Lysander before her nails can reach Helena's eyes.

- Missed grabs by the boys, and girls running under arms to continue the fight also can be funny.

- In the passage where Helena asks for help, " I pray you, though you mock me, gentlemen, Let her not hurt me . . . " (III, ii, 314–315), Helena could forget her outrage at all of them and flutter eyelids as she sidles up to Demetrius for his big, strong help.

Step-by-Step

1. Have students read aloud Section 4, lines 124–365.
2. Teach students how to create tableaus. A tableau is a teaching tool in which students pose in frozen and exaggerated positions to represent a significant part of a scene or to demonstrate a definition of a word. A student narrator explains the depiction and why it is important. This strategy reinforces student learning kinesthetically, as it adds another layer of understanding about characters and plot.

"I beseech you"

3. Direct students to create tableaus for the moments listed on the next page in the progression of the fight, to use as discussion points and help visual learners keep track of the plot. In each tableau, a different aspect of the conflict is shown. Here are three ways for you to set up the tableaus:
    - Students choose their own dramatic moments.
    - You read the tableau moments for each group.
    - Hand out the Tableau Cards printed on p. 100 to assign each group a dramatic moment.

4. Model this technique by choosing five students to demonstrate a tableau to the class. Using lines 242–244 with the four lovers, have Helena exaggerate a pained look on her face. Hermia looks astonished with her mouth wide open, and Demetrius and Lysander wink at each other. The student who is designated as narrator should first read the three-line passage and then explain the significance of this scene: "... counterfeit sad looks, / Make mouths upon me when I turn my back, / Wink each at other, hold the sweet jest up" (III, ii, 242–244). This moment shows that Helena thinks everyone is mocking her, although in the reality of the play, that is *not* what is occurring. Because of the potion, Demetrius is back in love with her and Lysander also loves her, but she doesn't believe them. Here are some tableau moments for students to create:

- Lines 258–261—Four lovers plus a narrator. Lysander and Demetrius try to convince Helena that each one loves her more. (Helena thinks that they have all joined to humiliate her. At this moment, she feels rage and is on the verge of tears.)
- Lines 270–271—Lysander and Hermia plus a narrator. Lysander tries to make Hermia let go of him after convincing her that he doesn't love her anymore. (Lysander doesn't want to appear to be connected to Hermia now that he loves Helena, but Hermia wants to assert her right to Lysander.)
- Lines 311–315—Four lovers plus a narrator. Hermia is about to attack Helena and scratch her eyes out. Helena might hide behind Demetrius for protection. (Helena still adores Demetrius even though she also is mad about what she thinks is his mockery. She exaggerates her fear of Hermia to have a moment with him. Hermia thinks her friend has been a traitor and stolen the love of Lysander.)
- Lines 356–358—Demetrius and Lysander plus a narrator. The two men vie to show who is the bravest and most committed to winning the rivalry for Helena. (Both boys want to prove they are manlier than the other. In their interest in outshining each other, they completely ignore Helena!)
- Lines 363–365—Helena and Hermia plus a narrator. Helena is running away from Hermia, who is completely confused by the entire situation. (Each girl has said exaggerated hurtful things to each other and now Helena is fearful and wants to get away from Hermia. Hermia cools off and is astonished by what is happening.)

5. Have students dramatize Section 4, lines 124–365.
6. Tell the summary of Section 5, lines 366–421 with Oberon and Puck. Discussion points for this section include:

- 🌸 Puck claims to have made innocent mistakes, "Believe me, king of shadows, I mistook" (III, ii, 368). Do you believe him? Why or why not?

- 🌸 Puck brings up the fact that dawn is approaching, which means that troubled ghosts must return to their graves. The dark aspects of death, including suicide, emerge in lines 402–409. Oberon quickly changes the subject, focusing on the brighter aspects of the spirit world. From this point forward in the play, notice other contrasts between life and death, light and dark, which exemplify the underside of the bright and frothy surface of this play. This foreshadows the final speeches of the play in Act V, scene i, lines 388–439.

Production Note: If you are producing *MSND*, your intermission should happen here, after Puck's last spell. Having staged *MSND* numerous times, I've solved a few of the problems in staging in different ways. One of the tricks is to have Lysander fall asleep downstage left (from the actor's point of view on stage), then Demetrius falls asleep on the downstage right corner of the playing area. After this, Helena enters and sleeps downstage right without seeing Demetrius, and lastly Hermia enters and sleeps downstage left. It is important that each couple is close enough to see each other when they wake in Act IV, but it must be done in a way that the girls can lie down and sleep without it seeming obvious that the boys are there. Depending on your circumstances, pillows or foliage can be used. If you have lights, they can go down slowly on this image of the sleeping Athenians, and the actors can disappear when the lights go to black. Then, after the intermission they resume their positions in the dark so that when the play resumes with Act IV, we are right where we left off at the end of Act III.

7. Give the summary of Section 6, lines 422 to the end. Read or act out from lines 440 to the end. Discussion points for the entire scene include:
    - 🌸 What effect do jealousy and disloyalty have on friendships?
    - 🌸 Predict what will happen next and if these friends and lovers will ever be able to forgive each other.
8. Give the Quiz on Act III of *A Midsummer Night's Dream.*

Writing About MSND

9. Journal Entry: For homework, have students write detailed diary entries in their journals from the perspective of the same character they chose at the end of Act II. Answer the prompt, "How do I feel tonight?" After they finish, have them make a brief entry from the point of view of their character's rival.

Doing the rival's entry will give them appreciation for (1) how each character has his or her own reality, point of view, and legitimacy as a human being, and (2) how skilled Shakespeare was in creating so many characters, each with powerful, valid, and yet opposing realities.

10. Extension: Students might enjoy finding some modern songs that focus on these same themes or parodies of the themes (e.g., "Stand by Your Man," sung by Tammy Wynette; "No One" sung by Alicia Keys; and of course, "Love Potion No. 9"). Let students bring the song ideas to class the next day and either sing a verse, play a recording, or show an Internet performance, and tell why they chose that song. They should make the connection between the song and one of the issues in *MSND*, including which character might sing it. This activity will help students explore these ideas in modern, relevant ways and look at a theme from different characters' perspectives.

Tableau Cards for the Fight Scene

1. Lines 258–261. Four lovers plus a narrator.

   Lysander and Demetrius try to convince Helena that each one loves her more.

2. Lines 270–271. Lysander and Hermia plus a narrator.

   Lysander tries to make Hermia let go of him after convincing her that he doesn't love her anymore.

3. Lines 311–315. Four lovers plus a narrator.

   Hermia is about to attack Helena and scratch her eyes out. Helena might hide behind Demetrius for protection.

4. Lines 356–358. Demetrius and Lysander plus a narrator.

   The two men vie to show who is the bravest and most committed to winning in the rivalry for Helena.

5. Lines 363–365. Helena and Hermia plus a narrator.

   Helena is running away from Hermia, who is completely confused by the entire situation.

Name: _____   Date: _____

Quiz on Act III of
A Midsummer Night's Dream

A. Vocabulary—Fill in the blanks with the appropriate vocabulary words that match the appropriate corresponding definitions/synonyms.

ouzel   gambol   fruitless   turn   gleek   sojourn   press   chronicle   abate   chid

1. _____   to make a joke, to jest

2. _____   skip, leap about

3. _____   cut short

4. _____   blackbird

5. _____   travel

6. _____   written up in histories

7. _____   scolded

8. _____   urge, push

9. _____   alter, change

10. _____   idle, empty

B. Short Answer

1. What are two ways that Shakespeare creates the magical world of the fairy kingdom?

_____

_____

_____

2. Why are Helena and Hermia arguing?

_____

_____

_____

3. When Quince says, "Bottom, thou are translated," what does he mean?

_____

_____

_____

4. What is Bottom's reaction to Titania's advances?

_____

_____

_____

Teacher's Answer Guide for Quiz on Act III of *A Midsummer Night's Dream*

A. Vocabulary

1. gleek
2. gambol
3. abate
4. ouzel
5. sojourn
6. chronicle
7. chid
8. press
9. turn
10. fruitless

B. Short Answer

1. Answers could include: lush, rich descriptions of the fairy world; the fairies' magic; Puck's ventriloquism; the fairies speak in a seven-meter line pattern when they use magic, which contrasts with the iambic pentameter.
2. Helena thinks that Hermia is cruelly mocking her, and being a mean and disloyal friend. Hermia is confused that Lysander is professing love to Helena, and Hermia thinks that Helena has stolen her love, Lysander.
3. He should have said, "thou are transformed," meaning that Bottom has been changed from a man into a beast.
4. He ignores her and banters with the fairies.

Chapter 4
Act IV

*I have had a most rare vision. I have had a dream
past the wit of man to say what a dream it was.*
—Bottom (IV, i, 214–216)

Act IV, Scene i

Objective: Students will read, interpret, and discuss Shakespeare's use of language, characters, and plot.

Vocabulary:

- ❧ *amiable*—loveable, agreeable (l. 2)
- ❧ *coy*—caress (l. 2)
- ❧ *amity*—friendship and peace (l. 91)
- ❧ *vaward*—vanguard, leading position (l. 109)
- ❧ *enmity*—hatred between enemies, hostility (l. 151)
- ❧ *stealth*—secretive, quiet, and covert so to avoid detection (l. 167)

Summary of Act IV, Scene i by Sections

Break up the reading/dramatizing of this scene into these four sections with a brief summary before students read or act out each section.

Characters: Bottom, Titania, Peaseblossom, Cobweb, Mustardseed

Summary of Section 1, lines 1–46: Titania continues to pamper Bottom, finally sending her fairies away so they can sleep together. Her rapture continues as she says, "O, how I love thee! How I dote on thee!" (IV, i, 46), just before falling asleep next to Bottom.

Characters: Oberon, Puck, Titania

Summary of Section 2, lines 47–106: Oberon tells Puck that recently he saw Titania in the woods mooning about with Bottom and succeeded in getting the boy to be his page. His last line in releasing her from the spell shows that all of his anger has gone: "Now, Titania, wake you, my sweet queen" (IV, i, 76). She awakes refreshed but appalled when she sees Bottom and realizes that her love for this monstrous creature was not just a dream. Puck removes the ass head from Bottom and Titania orders music to keep Bottom and the four lovers asleep. As the morning lark announces day, Oberon, Titania, and Puck depart.

Characters: Theseus, Hippolyta, Egeus, Lysander, Demetrius, Hermia, Helena

Summary of Section 3, lines 107–209: Theseus and Hippolyta enter the forest to spend their wedding morning hunting. They enjoy their conversation about hunting dogs they have each heard during past hunts throughout the ancient regions of Greece. Before they go farther, they see the waking lovers, and Egeus, who is a member of their party, spies his daughter and reiterates his intent for her to marry Demetrius. After Demetrius explains that he has changed his mind and wants to marry Helena, Theseus agrees and the court leaves. As the four lovers follow and exit, they explore their strange and otherworldly feelings about their night. Demetrius wonders if they are actually awake, " . . . It seems to me / That yet we sleep, we dream" (IV, i, 202–203).

Character: Bottom

Summary of Section 4, lines 210–229: Bottom is the last to wake, and at first he thinks that he has just fallen asleep in rehearsal and missed his cue, but as he remembers he says, "I have had a dream past the wit of man to say what dream it was" (IV, i, 215–216). Every time he almost says that he thought he was an ass, he stops himself from saying the word. He says that he will have Peter Quince write a ballad of the dream, "It shall be called, 'Bottom's Dream' because it hath no bottom" (IV, i, 225–226).

Titania and the fairies entertain Bottom

Step-by-Step

1. Give the summary for Section 1. Either have the students read this section for homework or read aloud together with students playing the different roles. Discuss with your class the following:

   🌸 **Titania's language is elaborate, sensual, and suggestive, yet Bottom appears more interested in food and sleep. Why do you think this is?** (She is the one filled with desire. He is now an ass, who is interested in eating donkey food and sleeping, as animals often are.)

2. Give the summary for Section 2. Have students dramatize the scene with Oberon and Titania in lines 41–106. Discussion points include:

   🌸 All of the action with the Indian boy takes place off stage. Even though it seems to be the key bone of contention between Oberon and Titania when we first meet them, it is quickly resolved when under enchantment she gives up the boy with no argument. **Why do you think Shakespeare did this?** (One possibility is that the Indian boy himself was not really what they were arguing about, but more a displacement of their mutual jealousy and insecurity about their previous relationships with Theseus and Hippolyta. Each one gained something—Oberon got his revenge and the boy, and Titania got the ecstasy of a night with a magical paramour.)

   🌸 **Notice the alternation between iambic pentameter and the seven-beat magical meter and when it occurs.** (In lines 72–75 once again we see a magical incantation as Oberon removes the magical spell from Titania's eyes. Although there is no incantation in lines 97–106, we find ourselves in that magical transitional space between night and morning when the fairies disappear.)

3. Tell the summary of Section 3, lines 107–209 and have students read it. Discussion points for this section include:

- ✿ We haven't learned much about Theseus and Hippolyta until this scene. We knew that he had won her in battle, but now we begin to see what they have in common. (Both love the outdoors, the drama of the hunt, and the musicality of the hounds.)

- ✿ **What are some of the musical images found in the conversation between Theseus and Hippolyta when they talk about hunting?**
  - My love shall hear the **music** of my hounds (IV, i, 110)
  - **musical** confusion / Of hounds and **echo** in conjunction (IV, i, 114–115)
  - I never heard / so **musical a discord**, such **sweet thunder** (IV, i, 121–122)
  - matched in mouth **like bells** (IV, i, 127)
  - A **cry more tunable** / Was never holloed to, nor **cheered with horn** (IV, i, 128– 129)

- ✿ Within this discussion, notice the contrasts and oxymorons Shakespeare writes (of hounds and echo in conjunction, musical a discord, sweet thunder, a cry more tunable).

- ✿ Although Hermia's choice of partner seemed to be a key factor in the play in Act I, now the problem is resolved in one line, "Egeus, I will overbear your will" (IV, i, 186). Why do you think this is? (On a plot level, Demetrius no longer wants to marry Hermia, so Egeus couldn't get his wish. But in the larger picture, it looks a lot like a McGuffin.)

- ✿ **When they are alone, how do the lovers describe their dream-like state; what are their perceptions?** They each describe out-of-focus, nebulous experiences in clear visual images. Demetrius ends by saying, "let us recount our dreams" (IV, i, 209).
  - "These things seem small and undistinguishable, / Like far-off mountains turnèd into clouds"—Demetrius (IV, i, 194–195)
  - "everything seems double"—Hermia (IV, i, 197)
  - "found Demetrius like a jewel, / Mine own and not mine own"—Helena (IV, i, 199–200)
  - "Are you sure / That we are awake? It seems to me / That yet we sleep, we dream"—Demetrius (IV, i, 201–203)

4. Tell the summary of Section 4.

> **Production Note:** The actor playing Bottom should stop himself and leave a tiny thoughtful pause each time Bottom almost says "ass" during the lines 217–219: "Methought I was—..." This will let the audience feel how odd Bottom feels in remembering the tactile memory of being half beast.

5. Dramatize Bottom's dream. Discussion points include:
   - Every sense is discombobulated as an aftermath of this dislocating dream-like experience. Find the textual evidence and compare Bottom's perceptions with that of the lovers. (See the Note to Teacher on p. 109.)

> **From the Director's Chair:** When Bottom decides to commission Quince to write up his "dream" and use it for the acting troupe, he shows he is a true man of the theatre—not wanting to waste any experience that can be used for his craft.

- **Discuss Bottom the weaver's name and why it is an appropriate name for this character.**
  - He comes from a lower rung of society—not the bottom, but not the court.
  - He is transformed into an ass, which has two definitions: a donkey, and a rear end or "bottom."
  - Another definition of the word *ass* is "an ignorant fellow, a perverse fool, a conceited dolt" (*OED*, 1971, p. 125).
  - Sometimes he behaves like a fool, an ass, a "bottom."
  - He is a weaver and a "bottom" was the name of the large spool at the base of a hand loom that was part of the weaver's trade, " a 'clew' or nucleus on which to wind thread" (*OED*, 1971, p. 254).
  - He also represents the bottomless or deepest nature of human beings that can be beast-like or bottomlessly spiritual.
  - Bottom "weaves" together the social hierarchies of the aristocrats and the workingmen, as he interacts with Theseus during the play-within-a-play.

Writing About MSND

6. Journal Entry: Have students rewrite Oberon's speech (IV, i, 47–76) in modern language. Encourage them to use their own expressions and everyday language. The next day, have several students share their versions with the class.

Note to Teacher: For those whose minds have a metaphysical bent, this next note may provide a profound morsel to examine about the deeper levels to Bottom's name. The brief lines called "Bottom's dream" are full of allusions to the Bible and to deeply spiritual matters and have been the source of much thinking about the concept of infinity or bottomlessness over the ages.

Bottom's dream

Bottom acknowledges that he cannot really understand what his dream means and says, "The eye of man hath not heard, the ear of man hath not seen, man's hand is not able to taste, his tongue to conceive, nor his heart to report what my dream was" (IV, i, 220–224). This seems to be another mixed-up word usage by Bottom, yet an audience conversant with the New Testament would have heard the parallels to I Corinthians 2:9. This Bible passage talks about the idea that people can't grasp all of the wonderful things God has prepared for those who believe in him, and that the spirit is always looking for the deep parts of God.

Recently, scholars have discovered that an earlier translation of the Bible adds a rich layer of understanding. If we imagine that the Geneva Bible, published in 1557 (7 years before Shakespeare's birth), was in Shakespeare's home when he was growing up, the wording reverberates even more with Bottom's name. In that version the passage ends, "For the spirit searches all things, yea, the bottom of God's secrets" (Rosenbaum, 2006, p. 16). Rosenbaum sums up this revelation with a provocative unanswerable question about Bottom the weaver's name, "Was Shakespeare thinking only of weavers' spools and butts and asses in naming one of his greatest characters Bottom? Or is there an allusion as well to the deepest, most bottomless mysteries of creation, 'the bottom of God's secrets?'" (p. 16).

Act IV, Scene ii

Objective: After reading and discussing Act IV, scene ii, students will compose a reflective writing piece that conveys insight, knowledge, and opinion through a double entry journal.

Materials:

- Act IV Vocabulary Words (p. 113)
- Venn Diagram: Comparing and Contrasting Two Characters (p. 114)

Vocabulary:

- *paramour*—a lover, especially one in a relationship with a married person (l. 12)
- *paragon*—someone who is the best example of something (l. 13)
- *discourse*—to formally speak about a subject at length (l. 29)

Summary of Act IV, Scene ii

Characters: Quince, Starveling, Flute, Snug, Bottom

Summary: While the mechanicals worry that Bottom has not arrived, they praise his talent and express a concern about the money he will lose by not performing. All of a sudden Bottom returns. He postpones telling them his miraculous tale, but makes sure to tell them practical matters for their upcoming performance.

> *From the Director's Chair:* There is a sweet loyalty among the players, which is illustrated in their conversation before Bottom reappears. You can almost hear Shakespeare's own owner/manager voice worrying about his actors and then, after Bottom arrives, telling the troupe how to prepare for that evening's performance.

Step-by-Step

1. Tell the summary of scene ii. Have students read the scene.

Discussion points:

- ✀ The reward of being chosen to do the play could be a lifetime pension for actors.
- ✀ Shakespeare was not only a playwright, he was also an actor and director. **Notice the practical theatrical advice Bottom gives to the other mechanicals in lines 34–45.** Find examples such as the following:
    - "Get your apparel together, good strings to your beards, new ribbons to your pumps" (IV, ii, 35–37). It was important that the beard strings don't break or the beard would fall off. The ribbons add decoration to their everyday shoes.
    - "Every man look o'er his part" (IV, ii, 37–38). Good actors who have had little rehearsal do a last-minute preparation of looking over lines.
    - " . . . let not him that plays the lion pare his nails, for they shall hang out for the lion's claws" (IV, ii, 40–41). He is thinking about an authentic look to give the part more realism. This is the purpose of theatrical make-up.
    - " . . . eat no onions nor garlic, for we are to utter sweet breath . . . " (IV, ii, 42–43). He is making sure that the actors don't have bad breath that would offend the audience.

2. Distribute the handout, Act IV Vocabulary Words, and for homework or in class, have students write a sentence with each one so that it is clear what the words mean in context.

3. Journal Entry: For homework, have students choose a quote or passage and write a double entry journal response to it. (See example on p. 59.)

4. Extension: Distribute the handout, Venn Diagram: Comparing and Contrasting Two Characters and have students select two characters from the worksheet and complete the Venn diagram. Allow time for students to discuss these the next day and have them posted during the Culminating Celebration.

Act IV Vocabulary Words

Directions: Select six of the following words and write a sentence with each one so that it is clear what the words mean in context. Script lines are listed after the words.

Example: "I'll see you *anon*," Cliff said to Alex, knowing that he would see his friend in the next class.

From Scene i:

❧ *amiable*—loveable, agreeable (l. 2)

❧ *coy*—caress (l. 2)

❧ *amity*—friendship and peace (l. 91)

❧ *vaward*—vanguard, early part (l. 109)

❧ *enmity*—hatred between enemies, hostility (l. 151)

❧ *stealth*—secretiveness, quiet, and covert behavior so to avoid detection (l. 167)

From Scene ii:

❧ *paramour*—a lover, especially one in a relationship with a married person (l. 12)

❧ *paragon*—someone who is the best example of something (l. 13)

❧ *discourse*—to formally speak about a subject at length (l. 29)

Name: _____

Date: _____

Venn Diagram: Comparing and Contrasting Two Characters

Directions: Choose **one** of the following pairs of characters and write their names on the lines. List the unique qualities of each character under their names in the circles. Put common qualities they share in the middle.

Bottom and Puck; Hippolyta and Titania; Helena and Hermia; Oberon and Theseus; Titania and Oberon

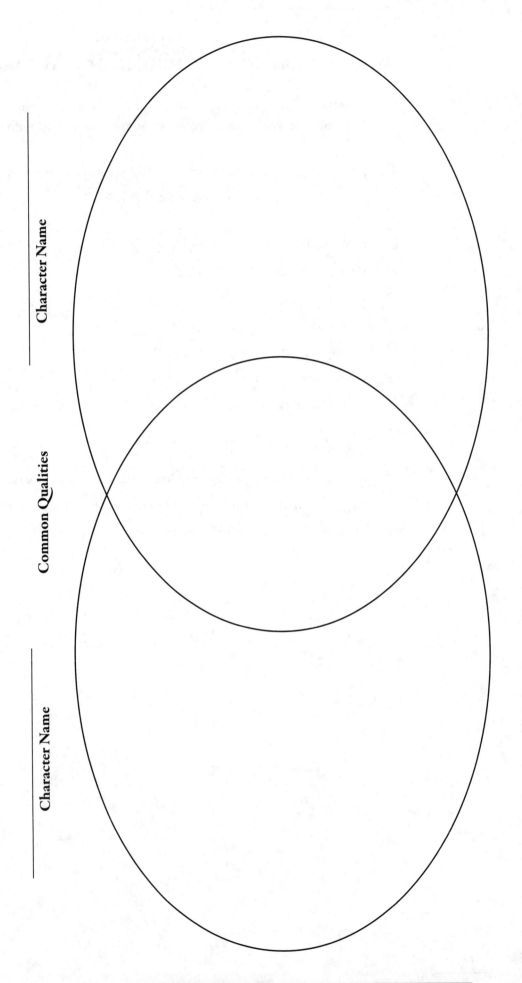

Character Name

Common Qualities

Character Name

Chapter 5
Act V

I will hear that play,
For never anything can be amiss
When simpleness and duty tender it.
—Theseus (V, i, 87–89)

Act V, Scene i

Objective: Students will dramatize sections of Act V and discuss how details of language develop characters and produce a dominant tone.

Vocabulary:

※ *dumb show*—a pantomime version of the play that follows

Summary of Act V by Sections

Characters: Hippolyta, Theseus, Philostrate, Lysander, Hermia, Demetrius, Helena

Summary of Section 1, lines 1–113: Theseus and Hippolyta enter discussing the story the lovers related. Theseus doesn't believe them, but ruminates about how lunatics, lovers, and poets (writers) all share the common thread of making something appear out of nothing. They are soon joined by Lysander and Hermia, and Demetrius and Helena, and choose a play for the entertainment celebrating their weddings. The goodwill that flows from Theseus's joy at the weddings spreads over into his discussions of imagination and of giving people the benefit of the doubt.

Characters: All of the above, plus Quince (Prologue), Bottom (Pyramus), Flute (Thisbe), Snout (Wall), Starveling (Moonshine), Snug (Lion)

Summary of Section 2, lines 114–387: This is the heart of the last act, the play-within-the-play. Peter Quince enters as the Prologue and the courtiers make comments that show their wit. He introduces the actors who act out a dumb show (pantomime) of the action of the play that is to follow. Pyramus (Bottom) enters first, followed by his forbidden sweetheart, Thisbe (Flute). Wall (Snout) comes next, separating the two sweethearts and showing the chink in the wall with his fingers held apart. Moonshine (Starveling) enters with a lantern and at last Lion (Snug) enters and shows how he will frighten Thisbe and maul her shawl with his mouth. After the dumb show, the play begins in earnest. Comments abound from the courtiers, and from Bottom when he sees fit to get out of character and discourse with the nobles. The humor comes from the mechanicals trying to be earnest and extremely dramatic while presenting this ridiculous play. After the play ends with its double suicide, the actors are rewarded. At midnight Theseus, Hippolyta, and all of the lovers exit to go off to their marriage beds.

Characters: Puck, Oberon, Titania, fairies

Summary of Section 3, lines 388–455: Puck enters the empty stage and talks about how it is the dead of night when dark spirits abound and only troubled souls are out in the world. Oberon, Titania, and their train enter and the tone changes as they lead the fairies in a dance of blessing. Oberon's blessing promises that these married couples shall not have children with birth defects. He and Titania will bless Theseus and Hippolyta's bed while other fairies are sent to bless the Athenian lovers. Puck remains and suggests that if the audience didn't like the play, they should consider it "but a dream" (V, i, 445). He ends by asking them to refrain from hissing at the actors—"'scape the serpent's tongue" (V, i, 450)—but instead to applaud—"give me your hands" (V, i, 454).

Fairies dance their blessings

From the Director's Chair: Your students may be surprised and delighted to learn that the music that often accompanies the beginning of Act V is very familiar to them. Mendelssohn's "Wedding March," which has accompanied countless Americans on their way to the altar, was written in 1842 as part of the incidental music for *A Midsummer Night's Dream.*

Step-by-Step

1. Summarize Section 1.
2. Do a close reading of the conversation between Hippolyta and Theseus as students read aloud or dramatize (see p. 119 for an example).
3. Summarize Section 2, the play-within-the-play.

Thisbe and Lion crack up off stage

Dramatizing, Understanding, and Discussing MSND

4. Have students act out the play-within-the-play, beginning with line 112. Discussion points include:
   - Some scholars think that *MSND* and *Romeo and Juliet* were written simultaneously. Although you are not studying *Romeo and Juliet* at the moment, it is worthwhile to note that almost the same tragedy with star-crossed lovers happens in both, but it is treated as comedy, not tragedy, in *MSND*. The theme of misunderstanding in love plays out in lighter variations in the romance of Hermia and Lysander.

CLOSE READING
Section 1 of Act V

HIPPOLYTA (V, i, 1) 'Tis strange, my Theseus, that these lovers speak of.	This is the first time Hippolyta directly addresses Theseus, using his name. Although she seemed quite cool to him in Act I, now that they have enjoyed each other's company in the hunting scene, she calls him, "my Theseus."
THESEUS (V, i, 2–23) More strange than true. I never may believe These antique fables, nor these fairy toys. Lovers and madmen have such seething brains, Such shaping fantasies, that apprehend More than cool reason ever comprehends. The lunatic, the lover, and the poet Are of imagination all compact. One sees more devils than vast hell can hold: That is the madman. The lover, all as frantic, Sees Helen's beauty in a brow of Egypt. The poet's eye, in a fine frenzy rolling, Doth glance from heaven to earth, from earth to heaven, And as imagination bodies forth The forms of things unknown, the poet's pen Turns them to shapes and gives to airy nothing A local habitation and a name. Such tricks hath strong imagination That, if it would but apprehend some joy, It comprehends some bringer of that joy. Or in the night, imagining some fear, How easy is a bush supposed a bear!	Theseus doesn't believe the stories. Look closely at lines 12–18 where Shakespeare is saying, "Look how I write!" Shakespeare has Theseus describe the writer's process as one in which lovers, madmen, and poets have much in common. Shakespeare created all of the characters and voices in the play—characters that can be viewed from different perspectives. The vicissitudes of "the lover" are demonstrated in the Athenian boys who at one time see Hermia as the most beautiful girl in the world, then another time see Helena as the greatest beauty. He created Bottom, who might be seen as a "madman" (l. 10) or crazy man, and who was supposed to be a monster. The OED (1971) defines lunacy as "intermittent insanity such as was formerly supposed to be brought about by the changes in the moon" (p. 1678). Shakespeare acknowledges that it is the writer ("poet's pen," l. 16) who gives form, voice, and setting to imagined creatures and events. This passage is so well known as describing Shakespeare's feeling about writing that the OED uses it in defining "poet" as a "writer in verse" (p. 2220).
HIPPOLYTA (V, i, 24–28) But all the story of the night told over, And all their minds transfigured so together, More witnesseth than fancy's images And grows to something of great constancy, But, howsoever, strange and admirable.	She believes the stories because their bizarre accounts of what happened in the night are too similar ("all their minds transfigured so together," l. 25) to have been made up. The phrase, "More witnesseth than fancy's images" (l. 26) lets the audience know that Hippolyta recognizes that what happened to the lovers is beyond the imaginary. Hippolyta uses the word *transfigured* for what happened to the lovers. During that same night Bottom was changed, transfigured, and transformed. Although not so dramatically, Hippolyta seems to be transformed in her connection with Theseus.

Production Note: In a production, feel free to milk Pyramus's death and make sure that the "die, die, die, die, die" (V, i, 322) section is timed so that there is one more left after the audience thinks he has gone down for the last time. He should pop up one last time for one last huge laugh.

You will want a few props for the Pyramus and Thisbe play. Here are some simple suggestions:

- A piece of cardboard painted to look like a stone wall and hung around Wall's neck with twine or rope makes a good costume.

- Thisbe needs a hanky to drop and it can be a funny sight gag if one side is clean and the other side "bloody." Then Pyramus, with a flourish, can display the bloody side to the audience when he is certain Thisbe has been killed by Lion.

- A simple lantern will do for Moonshine, or one hung from a pole if you prefer that effect.

- Try to locate a "Juliet dagger" (a trick dagger with a retractable blade, now available at novelty shops or online). It is a great item to use in the endless death scene of Pyramus, allowing him to stab himself all over to great comic effect.

- Please don't feel constrained to be modest in padding Thisbe. Over the years I've noticed that the larger the chest on this cross-dressed character, the more laughs it gets.

- One purpose for this play-within-the-play is simply comedic enjoyment. There is speculation that *MSND* may have been written as the entertainment for an actual wedding. Note that it is scripted to include dances and music, which is congruent for an Elizabethan wedding celebration.

- The mechanicals, who speak in prose, have written their play in iambic pentameter that is quite choppy. They have lots of internal rhymes, a couplet at the end of the prologue, and alliteration. They have tried to put in every kind of literary device, but much of it doesn't make sense, and punctuation is in the wrong places. They tried to use the elegant blank verse, but because they are unfamiliar, it comes across very rough, just like they are. Even visually the text looks out of kilter, unlike the other iambic pentameters.

- **In what ways are there parallels between the story of Pyramus and Thisbe to the characters in *MSND*?**
    - Pyramus and Thisbe were forbidden by their parents to be together, and Hermia and Lysander were forbidden by Egeus to marry.
    - Pyramus misinterpreted Thisbe's bloody cloak to mean her death; Puck mistook Lysander for Demetrius and put the nectar on the

wrong man's eyes; Titania also mistook Bottom for a handsome lover.

- The theme of misunderstanding in love plays out in lighter variations in the romance of Hermia and Lysander.

When Theseus chuckles, "Our sport shall be to take what they mistake" (V, i, 96), notice the play on the contrasting words, "**take**" and "mis**take**."

The mechanicals' misuse of language enhances the comedy of the tragedy of Pyramus and Thisbe. What were some of their mistakes and mix-ups?

- "I see a voice!" (V, i, 204; instead of *hear* a voice)
- "...I can hear my Thisbe's face" (V, i, 205; instead of *see* my Thisbe's face)
- "Sweet Moon, I thank thee for thy sunny beams" (V, i, 287; confused *sun* and *moon*).
- "Since lion vile hath here deflowered my dear" (V, i, 307; instead of *devoured*, also it was a bawdy joke).
- "... to see the Epilogue or to hear a Bergomask dance ..." (V, i, 369–370; mixes up *see* and *hear*)

Theseus speaks in prose for the first time in line 372–379. Why?

- When Theseus speaks prose with Bottom, he shows his respect for the common man in using their common language.

The mechanicals triumph

6. Tell the summary of Section 3. Do a close reading and analysis of lines 388–455 such as that on pp. 123–124.

Writing About MSND

7. Journal Entry: Choose one of the following two prompts:

❧ Recall or invent a dream of your own. Describe it using some of the following terms: ephemeral, blurred vision, insubstantial, just beyond reach, or edge of consciousness.

❧ Write a blessing for yourself, as you enter a new stage of your life, just as Oberon blesses the couples. You could use a real or imagined circumstance, such as going off to college, undertaking a new job, taking on new responsibilities as the leader of a club or organization, or getting married.

Happy lovers full of joy and mirth

CLOSE READING
Section 3 of Act V

PUCK (V, i, 388–407)

Now the hungry lion roars,
   And the wolf behowls the moon,
Whilst the heavy plowman snores,
   All with weary task fordone.
Now the wasted brands do glow,
   Whilst the screech-owl, screeching loud,
Puts the wretch that lies in woe
   In remembrance of a shroud.
Now it is the time of night
   That the graves, all gaping wide,
Every one lets forth his sprite
   In the church-way paths to glide.
And we fairies, that do run
   By the triple Hecate's team
From the presence of the sun,
   Following darkness like a dream,
Now are frolic. Not a mouse
   Shall disturb this hallowed house.
I am sent with broom before,
   To sweep the dust behind the door.

The lovers have all gone off to bed, but Puck has no sweet images of lovers. Instead, he speaks of the dark and despairing spirits and the ghosts of late night. Souls in Purgatory—between Heaven and Hell—roam at night before returning to their graves at dawn.

Fairies that follow the dark night mistress of the supernatural also are out frolicking. Puck's only admonition is that not even a mouse should disturb the house.

Puck often speaks of dark and scary images. Which ones do you notice?

Hungry lion, wolf behowls, screech-owl, wretch lies in woe, shroud, and graves gaping wide are just a few.

Why does Shakespeare have Puck bring out this dark side?

Life was not easy in Elizabethan England and many people had experienced the difficulties and traumas in life, with the Black Plague and other diseases. Puck brings out the realities and fears of many people. Many Elizabethans still followed folk practices to avoid the ill effects of dangerous spirits.

The last line, "To sweep the dust behind the door," suggests what?

It suggests that the dirt is not really gone, just out of sight for a while; perhaps problems will recur.

One of a "puck's" traditional jobs was keeping the house clean.

OBERON (V, i, 408–413)

Through the house give glimmering light,
   By the dead and drowsy fire.
Every elf and fairy sprite,
   Hop as light as bird from brier,
And this ditty after me,
Sing and dance it trippingly.

TITANIA (V, i, 414–417)

First rehearse your song by rote,
To each word a warbling note.
Hand in hand, with fairy grace,
Will we sing and bless this place.

Notice the mood swing when Oberon speaks. It is another sharp contrast from Puck's dark tone into a lighter blessing with his first line, "Through the house give glimmering light" (l. 408).

What meter is Oberon speaking in?

Seven beats per line, as we have seen in magic or special blessings.

Oberon and Titania gather the fairies to visit the wedding chambers and bless them with song and dance. Titania also is light and positive, and like Oberon, she speaks in seven beats.

Close Reading, Continued

OBERON (V, i, 418–439)
Now, until the break of day,
Through this house each fairy stray,
To the best bride-bed will we,
Which by us shall blesséd be,
And the issue there create
Ever shall be fortunate.
So shall all the couples three
Ever true in loving be,
And the blots of Nature's hand
Shall not in their issue stand.
Never mole, harelip, nor scar,
Nor mark prodigious, such as are
Despiséd in nativity,
Shall upon their children be.
With this field-dew consecrate
Every fairy take his gait,
And each several chamber bless,
Through this palace, with sweet peace.
And the owner of it blest,
Ever shall in safety rest.
Trip away. Make no stay.
Meet me all by break of day.
	Titania and Oberon bless their rivals' bed, and ensure that their babies will not be monsters.
	Beginning with "And the blots of Nature's hand" what strikes you as odd about this blessing?
	    In the blessings, more emphasis is given to avoiding misfortune than bringing good fortune. Perhaps this is an echo of so many years of plague sweeping England with misfortune.
	    Or, they don't emphasize how exceptional and wonderful their children should be, but rather what they shouldn't be. Could it be that a few sparks of jealousy still remain and they can't give them a full, whole-hearted blessing?
	    Oberon orders the other fairies to bless the other lovers' beds.

PUCK (Lines 440–455) If we shadows have offended, Think but this and all is mended: That you have but slumbered here While these visions did appear. And this weak and idle theme, No more yielding but a dream, Gentles, do not reprehend. If you pardon, we will mend. And, as I am an honest Puck, If we have unearnèd luck Now to 'scape the serpent's tongue, We will make amends ere long. Else the Puck a liar call. So good night unto you all. Give me your hands, if we be friends, And Robin shall restore amends.	All of the fairies leave, except for Puck, who gives the final epilogue. As in many of the scenes of the mechanicals rehearsing their play, Shakespeare ends *MSND* with another wink to the trade of show business. At the end of *MSND* he actually addresses the audience directly through Puck, expressing his hope that they will not hiss ("serpent's tongue"; l. 450) and instead will applaud ("Give me your hands"; l. 454) his latest play.

124   *A Midsummer Night's Dream*

Chapter 6
Culminating Celebration

Give me your hands, if we be friends
—Puck (V, i, 454)

Culminating Celebration

Objectives: To showcase students' learning throughout the study of *MSND*, students will:

- dramatize a favorite scene with a group of peers, and write an original prologue in iambic pentameter to introduce the scene;
- use Elizabethan language in a creative way by writing sweet-talk phrases and participating in a Sweet-Talk Challenge;
- research and prepare some foods that were common in Shakespeare's time; and
- write essays demonstrating their capacity to communicate knowledge, opinions, and insights through a clear thesis and effective organization of supporting ideas.

Note to Teachers: Preparations for the culminating celebration day will take place a few days prior to the celebration, as students plan their scenes to dramatize, write their iambic pentameter prologues, and create sweet-talk phrases. When they are ready, put it all together on this final day (or days) of celebration. It is likely that this will take several days, depending on how many events you choose to include. Enjoy and celebrate your students' creativity! Showcase student journals, Venn diagrams, visual displays, and any other assignments that resulted in products.

Step-by-Step

1. Dramatize a favorite passage. Have groups of students choose their favorite scene from *MSND*, rehearse it in their groups, and plan inventive costumes. Each group will introduce its scene with a prologue that they have written in iambic pentameter. You can either allow time for this assignment in class or assign it as homework.
2. Participate in a Sweet-Talk Challenge. Have students finalize their sweet-talk phrases, select their best ones and participate in the Sweet-Talk Challenge. If they don't already have The Elizabethan Sweet-Talk Challenge handout in their binders, distribute it to them (p. 21). Here are two ways you might set this up:
   - In an individual competition, each student rates the other students as they present, and the student with the highest score wins. Rating could be done on Puck's Elizabethan scale: hisses (the "serpent's tongue") vs. applause ("give me your hands").

❧ Working in teams, students choose their best one and are judged by an outside panel of judges (other staff members who are on a break).

3. Sample foods. Have students research the food from the Elizabethan period and bring in some savory dishes for the class to enjoy (but no mead!).

References

American Alliance for Theatre and Education. (n.d.). *The national standards for theatre education, grades 9–12.* Retrieved June 16, 2008, from http://www.aate.com/9-12Standards.html

College Board: Advanced Placement Program. (2007). *English language and composition, English literature and composition: Course description.* Princeton, NJ: Author. Retrieved December 4, 2007, from http://apcentral.collegeboard.com/apc/public/repository/52272_apenglocked5_30_4309.pdf

Crystal, D. (2004). *The history of English.* Retrieved on May 9, 2008, from http://www.davidcrystal.com/DC_articles/English6.pdf

Crystal, D. (2005a). *Pronouncing Shakespeare: The Globe experiment.* New York: Cambridge University Press.

Crystal, D. (2005b). *Performing the tongue that Shakespeare spoke.* Retrieved on May 9, 2008, http://www.davidcrystal.com/DC_articles/Shakespeare4.pdf.

Greenblatt, S. (2004). *Will in the world: How Shakespeare became Shakespeare.* New York: W. W. Norton.

Joseph, B. (1980) *Acting Shakespeare.* New York: Theatre Arts Books. (Original work published 1969)

Lace, W. W. (1995). *Social classes in Shakespeare's England: Shakespeare & his times.* Retrieved February 16, 2008, from http://www.brandonsd.mb.ca/crocus/library/shakespeare.htm

National Council of Teachers of English. (n.d.). *Standards for the English language arts.* Retrieved January 18, 2008, from http://www.ncte.org/about/over/standards/110846.htm

Oxford English dictionary, Compact edition. (1971). Glasgow, Scotland: Oxford University Press.

Perkawis, U. (n.d.). *Pawartos Jawi.* Retrieved May 9, 2008, from http://www.artindonesia.org/pawartos_jawi_underaningperkawis_dialect.htm

Rackin, P. (2005). *Shakespeare and women.* New York: Oxford University Press.

Reading notes scoring guide. (2004). Retrieved March 31, 2008, from http://www.warrenlocal.k12.oh.us/whs/HSProjects/SUMMER/ap4/readingnotesrubric.pdf

Rosenbaum, R. (2006). *The Shakespeare wars: Clashing scholars, public fiascoes, palace coups.* New York: Random Books.

Shakespeare, W. (1993/2004). *A midsummer night's dream* (B. A. Mowat & P. Werstine, Eds.). New York: Washington Square Press.

Smith, L. B. (1967). *The horizon book of the Elizabethan world.* New York: American Heritage.

Teaching Resources

Books

Cullum, A. (1995). *Shakespeare in the classroom.* Parsippany, NJ: Fearon Teacher Aids.

Cullum, A., & Almeida, D. (2000). *Push back the desks: A recipe for instruction.* North Billerica, MA: Curriculum Associates.

Onions, C. T. (1977). *A Shakespeare glossary* (2nd ed.). Oxford, England: Oxford University Press.

Films

Dieterie, W., & Reinhardt, M. (1935). *A midsummer night's dream* (Motion picture). United States: Warner Bros. Pictures.

Gund, C. (Producer). (2005). *A touch of greatness film documentary: A great American teacher and the lives he influenced* (Television broadcast). New York: PBS.

Hoffman, M. (Director). (1999). *A midsummer night's dream* (Motion picture). United States: Fox Searchlight Pictures.

Music

Mendelssohn, F. (1843). *Wedding march.* (Use any recording.)

About the Authors

Kathryn L. Johnson teaches in the School of Education at the University of Rhode Island. With a lifelong love of literature and language, Kay is a writer, a calligrapher, and a bookbinder of original, one-of-a-kind books. She lives in rural Rhode Island with her husband and two teenage sons. This is her fourth publication with Prufrock Press.

Laurie Heineman is an Emmy Award-winning actress who is the theatre teacher at St. Andrew's School in Rhode Island. She has led her "Playing with Shakespeare" workshops as enrichment for students, professional development for teachers, team-building for corporate leaders, and as pure enjoyment for library patrons and party-goers throughout New England. Laurie brings her passion and fun-loving spirit to the Bard's plays as she joyfully engages people of all ages. She and her husband are the parents of three wonderful children.

Workshops, conference presentations, and other related consulting may be arranged by contacting lauriehei@cox.net with "workshop" as the subject.